DESIGNER ORIGAMI

With origami, almost anything is possible! This artwork was created by Matthew Gardiner using textiles and 3D printing, in a process known as Oribotics.

ABOUT DESIGNER ORIGAMI

Artists have been using origami, the art of paper folding, to breathe life into paper for centuries. But origami is no longer limited to paper. These days origami uses many different materials and this book shows you some of the extraordinary things that origami can create. The introduction gives an overview, offering detailed and fascinating information on the science behind origami. Readers should feel free to jump right into the sections on origami making or read the introduction at any time for a behind-the-scenes look at the world of origami. Each of the step-by-step sections offers practical examples, many using materials other than paper, to create jewellery, fashion, lighting, decoration and animal displays. You will be amazed at what you can create through origami!

The author, Matthew Gardiner, is an artist, researcher and origamist whose artworks combine folding with robotics, lighting, networks and design.

Dedicated to my two precious jewels.

PURE ORIGAMI

ORIGAMI PURISM

Origami purists believe that the origamist must use a single sheet of paper, and should only use folds to create their work. Many people struggle to believe that a complex origami work can be created within these parameters. You might think that this restriction would limit origami designs to simple shapes and paper toys. However, the boom in origami in the latter 1900s proved that this restriction can yield any conceivable design. The only limits are the imagination, innovation and patience of the origamist.

The square shape of origami paper is often considered to be the ideal starting point for an origami model, but of course origami can be made from any shape you like. Some artists begin with equilateral triangles, silver rectangles (1:√2), ISO 216 International standard A-format paper sizes such as A4, or even hexagons (six-sided shapes), octagons (eight-sided shapes), circles and even more exotic forms. The tendency is to have a known geometrical ratio, which can simplify the design process. Take for instance the problem of making folds in equal divisions across a sheet of paper. A square is the ideal starting point when folding a grid. Similarly, starting with a hexagon is a simple way to achieve a tessellated grid of triangles.

The square is popular in origami because the ratio of having equal sides (or 1:1) makes the maths easier. The bird base, with four even-length flaps and one short flap, matches the shape of many animals, and is simple to fold from a square. The angles of 90°, 45°, 22.5° and even 60°, 30° and 15° are all very easily folded from a square. Most people don't realise that they are actually doing mathematics each time they fold a sheet of paper.

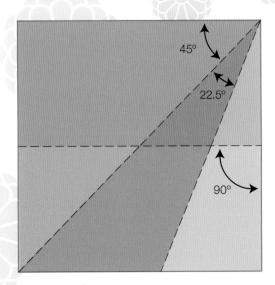

Square paper is popular in origami because we can quickly find useful angles using only folds.

The use of square shapes in origami is less a rule and more an approach made popular by its practicality and familiarity. In fact, any shape can be used for origami.

ORIGAMI IN OTHER DISCIPLINES

When used in fields such as fashion, industrial design and architecture, the term 'origami' often implies folding rather than reflecting the literal translation of origami: fold (ori) paper (gami). For example, a fashion designer might say that they made an origami dress, when they actually mean an origami-inspired dress. The designer uses folding techniques borrowed from origami to inspire their design, but breaks with origami purism due to the design requirements of the dress. Factors such as the fabric they are using and the organic rather than geometric nature of the human form will influence the shape of the material, and the design will most likely require cuts as well as folds. Perhaps the only people concerned about origami purism are those origamists working with paper.

Many people love the intellectual challenges posed by the restrictions of origami purism. Other disciplines, however, encounter plenty of different challenges when using origami. In later chapters we will use some 'impure' origami techniques, such as making a few cuts, using glue or putting stitches in fabric, but, where possible and practical, we'll keep to purism to demonstrate the sheer beauty of folded forms.

Above: Ananas scarf (see page 5 of the Fashion section) is an origami pattern pressed into a polyester textile.
Below: Masu pixel (see page 10 of the Lighting section) is a grid layout of coloured masu boxes that can be backlit with LED lighting.

THE SCALE OF FOLDS

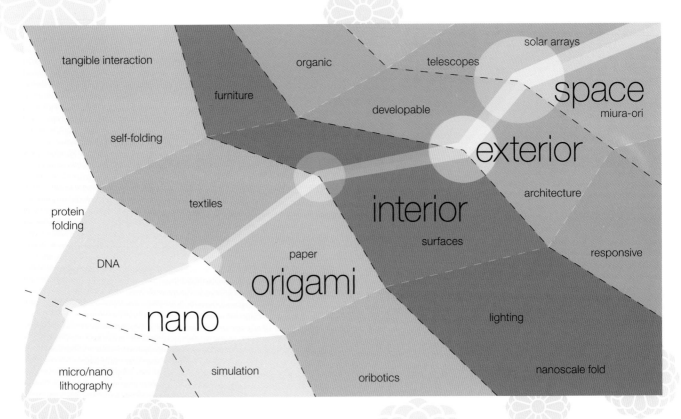

This image was first presented during a keynote lecture to computer scientists, designers and artists at a conference in Canada on tangible computing with the topic of 'fold/unfold' to help explain just how diverse folding actually is.

Folding is not just something that can be done with hands and paper. We can see folds at all scales, in nature and in technology. From DNA origami (folding strands of DNA into complex shapes) to unfolding space telescopes, origami and its associated science has opened up infinite possibilities and inspiration for artists, designers and engineers. The image above is an abstract map giving an overview of other fields associated with folding. Let's walk through the scale areas one by one, from the tiniest up to the largest scales.

NANOSCALE

Nanoscale folds are the tiniest folds possible. These folds are often used in science, and are leading to extraordinary new discoveries. Since the discovery that DNA has very specific folding patterns, a whole area of science has been devoted to studying these patterns. A DNA sequence has only one shape that it can fold into. In March 2006 *Nature* magazine featured DNA origami as the cover story. The key researcher, Paul W. K. Rothemund, had discovered that it was possible to fold DNA into specific shapes by mixing a strand of DNA with smaller strands that are programmed to connect and fold at certain locations. His team used the DNA's self-assembling process to create tiny images, including a copyright symbol and a smiley face.

A scientific research project founded at www.fold.it uses crowd-sourced problem solving – a method of using the collective brain power of the world – by making a game out of working out how to fold certain proteins. Their tagline is 'Solve Puzzles for Science'. The study is investigating whether human pattern recognition and puzzle-solving abilities are more efficient than computer

programs and, if so, aims to teach these strategies to computers so that they can fold proteins even faster. Proteins are used in almost all of the processes inside the human body. If researchers can discover their shapes, it may be possible to design proteins that can perform specific functions, such as attacking diseased cells and leaving healthy cells unharmed. In 2012 a research study showed that a high percentage of cancer cells were destroyed by their designer protein, and the healthy cells were left untouched. This new frontier of medical science has been made possible by understanding folds at the tiniest of scales.

Cascade water wall (see page 30 of the Decoration section) is a decorative form made from interlocking waterbomb units.

Matthew Gardiner's *Oribotics* at Tokyo Design Touch in 2010.

ORIGAMI SCALE

Paper is a human-scale medium. It is rarely larger than a human, except at the mass-production stage, at which point it is cut and kept on rolls that confine it to human scale. Objects at this scale are things we can fold and hold with our bare hands. This includes traditional origami, objects made from folded paper and folded textiles. This book is all about the origami scale of folding, and later chapters include many examples of the ideas explained here. The origami scale includes a vast range of folded forms. The number of origami models in the world went from about 200 known traditional models to hundreds of thousands in just a few decades. Artists use textiles and 3D printing to build robotic origami artworks, known as Oribotics. Fashion designers like Issey Miyake use folds and pleats in their fashion to generate new aesthetics for daily life. Designs such as the Bao Bao bag have proven incredibly popular. Folds, better known as pleating, have quite a history in fashion. From Scottish kilts to French haute couture, fashion has made use of pleating for centuries. Chris K. Palmer, in his book *Shadowfolds*, describes a new method of creating complex tessellated patterns in fabric, predominantly silk. This stylistic device can be used for clothing, but also for décor such as window treatments, lighting and interior decoration.

Oribotics looks towards the possibilities of self-folding systems. Researchers including Erik Demaine have shown that it is possible to engineer a self-folding system – a sheet of paper that folds itself on command. The team builds a complex prototype, using shape memory alloys for the hinges, silicon as a flexible base material, magnets to hold the finished folds in place and some algorithms to determine the optimum way to fold a given shape. They demonstrated a boat and a plane produced in this way in an academic paper published in 2010.

The diamond-cut can was introduced by Kirin Brewery into a line of drinks called Chuhai in 2001. This use of the Yoshimura pattern was a spin-off from research under Koryo Miura at the ISAS (Institute of Space and Aeronautical Science) in Japan. A detail of the pattern is shown here.

The M60 wrap (see page 9 of the Fashion section), a variation of the miura-ori, is an example of a complex pleat pressed into fabric.

Ars Electronica presented 'Create your World' at the 2011 Venice Biennale for Children. The furniture was designed by Linz-based Ars Electronica Futurelab, Gerald Priewasser, and created by PappLab. The entire exhibition design was fabricated from folded cardboard.
Photo courtesy: Ars Electronica

INTERIOR SCALE

The possibilities origami presents for surfaces, lighting, furniture and interior structure are quite open-ended and beautiful. You will find examples of lighting and decoration in later chapters. Designers are beginning to create furniture from paper and cardboard. A company in Linz, Austria, called PappLab (pappe meaning cardboard and lab for laboratory) constructed the furniture for the 2011 Ars Electronica Festival entirely from recyclable cardboard. The team had templates that they marked onto the large sheets and cut out by hand. They then folded and stapled the furniture together. The results were lightweight, strong, durable, beautiful and eco-friendly.

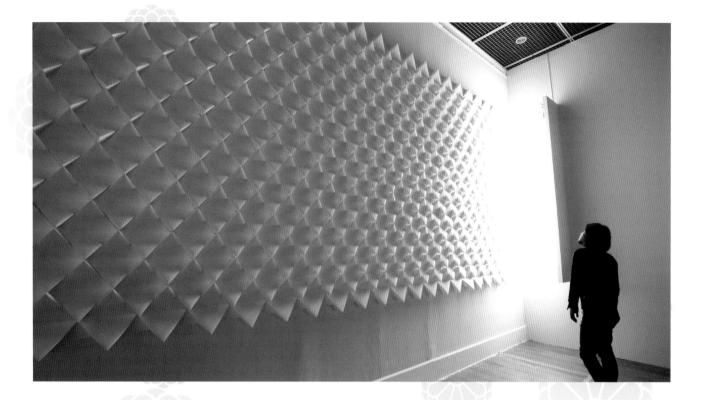

Creating textured surfaces from plastics and papers is not a new idea, but using algorithms to create variance in the pattern is. Artworks such as *nano-scale-fold*, as shown in the image above, take a simple folded pattern and introduce one variable: the height of the folded module.

The artwork above was created using software to calculate the fold pattern and a Techno Origami process with a laser to create the 450 sheets to be folded and wall-mounted. The lighting of the artwork varies over time – the soft LED lights on each side of the work fade up and down, like a rising and setting sun, dramatically altering the viewer's perception of the surface geometry. Light and shadow are commonly used to enhance the appearance of folds.

A 7 x 3-metre (23 x 9.8-foot) installation of *nano-scale-fold* by Matthew Gardiner, exhibited at the Museum of Contemporary Art in Taipei, completely fills the viewer's vision with a folded landscape that could, using nanoscale engineering technology, be manufactured to fit on a pinhead, one million times smaller. Photo courtesy: MOCA Taipei.

INTRODUCTION
THE SCALE OF FOLDS

Hideo Yasui gives deep consideration to origami in his architectural concept for Hiroshi Senju Museum Karuizawa, Japan: 'I aimed to give birth to infinite possibility in the museum, just as one piece of paper could be shaped to any possible form by human hands.'

EXTERIOR SCALE

The exterior scale is mostly seen in architecture. The increasing use of folded patterns in architecture is due to advances in architectural design tools. Visionaries such as Ron Resch were patenting folded designs as proposed architectural works as early as the mid-1960s, and R. Buckminster Fuller patented incredible innovations involving the application of folded surfaces to cover his geodesic domes from the 1940s onwards. However, the present-day architect has a clear advantage due to the availability of computer-aided design tools. Modern architectural design benefits from computational tools such as Rhino and plug-ins like Kangaroo and Grasshopper, leading to advances in architectural complexity.

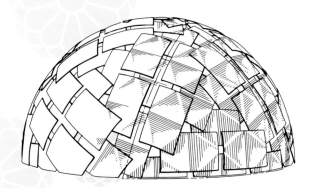

R. Buckminster Fuller's 1957 invention of a self-strutted geodesic plydome, shown above, uses gentle bends to guide the construction of one of his famous domes. The patent says, 'The flat sheets become both roof and beam, both wall and column and in each case the braces as well.'

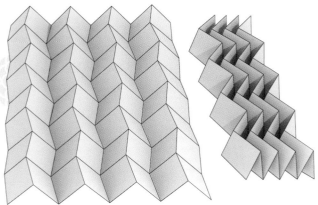

Since its use in space applications, the miura-ori has developed into an extensible paper display, especially useful for maps. It needs only one hand to open. When compared to opening a normally folded map, the design is a stroke of genius.

SPACE SCALE

Origami principles can also be applied when designing objects to be used in space. Not many people get the chance to work on a space program. Emeritus Koryo Miura had the opportunity to work at ISAS (the Institute of Space and Astronautical Science), now known as JAXA (Japanese Aerospace Exploration Agency). Koryo Miura is well-known for his discovery of the miura-ori, a folded pattern deduced and optimised through mathematical analysis. Through origami and folded systems he discovered engineering solutions for satellite design. Miura tackled problems such as designing compact telescopes and solar arrays, making them lightweight, and designing them so they can extend and contract in orbit using as little power as possible. There was only one chance to get it right, as once the satellite was launched there was no touching it again. Miura described a system that unfolded in orbit, powered by stored kinetic energy. Design efforts such as Miura's were small folds on paper, but represented a giant leap into space for origami.

PAPER AND TOOLS

QUALITY OF PAPER

A significant change to origami since the 1900s has been the focus on the quality of the paper. Commercially produced paper is generally not intended as a fine art material. It fades, and turns brittle with age, often because of the chemicals used in the process, but also because inexpensive fibre stock is of a lower quality. Surprisingly few origami artists have taken the time to learn the chemistry and the art of paper-making. Even when buying high-quality paper, the choices of archival, colourfast papers of suitable colours, textures and weights is quite limited. A significant exception is the paper created by Origamido Studio. Co-founders Michael LaFosse and Richard Alexander, from the United States, produce custom archival and colourfast folding papers

Handmade Origamido® papers.

known as Origamido® paper. The 'do' at the end of Origamido is a Japanese word ending meaning 'path', 'journey' or 'way', so 'Origamido' means 'paper-folding way', or, more poetically, 'lifelong journey of the paper-folding artist'.

LaFosse has been making his own paper since 1970, and Alexander since 2003. Their studio gallery has countless historical works folded by others many years ago, and most of the pieces folded from other papers have faded and cracked.

I had the pleasure of meeting them when they were special guests at Folding Australia 2009. They brought some of their handmade paper to the convention and I had the chance to observe and use the paper. The qualities of Origamido® paper are quite distinct from commercial papers. The paper is extremely thin and strong and, as it is formulated specifically for wet-folding, it is able to absorb water without the usual fibre separation and resulting weakness.

The paper has a wonderful crispness that holds a fold very well. Origamido® custom papers are generally pigmented, mostly with ground inorganics integrated into the fibres. Most commercial origami papers, on the other hand, are firstly made white before the colour, often a fugitive dye, is applied to the surface. Origamido® paper is made using only fine artist-quality colour pigments mixed with, and bonded directly into, premium pulp. While regular paper with printed dye inks can fade over time, the integration of the more chemically stable pigments into high-quality fibres means that Origamido® papers are permanent and colourfast.

its fibres. The length of the fibres makes it more resistant to breaking, as the fibres intersect and bind together across a larger area. Consider a paper with short fibres, such as toilet paper. It is so soft because the fibres are extremely short, and so it breaks very easily. Paper quality is vitally important, both during the folding process – will it hold up to the folds that will be made – and afterwards – will it last for decades, or even centuries, as a work of art?

ELEPHANT HIDE

Elephant hide is a mill paper that is popular among origamists. It is made by a German manufacturer, Zanders GmBH. Known in German as 'elefantenhaut', it is a strong paper that can be folded and unfolded many times without weakening and tearing. This resistance to tearing is an attribute admired by origamists who make complex works with many pre-creases, such as tessellations. The paper's strength comes from

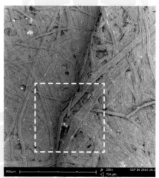

A magnified image showing a valley fold in elephant hide. In the detail on the right-hand side we see just one or two fibres – note the length – separating along the fold line.

MATHEMATICS

The study, or perhaps even science, of origami has radically expanded in the past 30 years. This has led to significant developments in our understanding of folds. Where designers of the past relied on intuition, creativity and trial and error, today's designers have the advantage of mathematical methods and computation. The beginning of the Origami, Science, Mathematics and Education conferences marked a shift towards a deeper understanding of origami maths and science. The conferences bring together people from around the world who present their research and inspire each other to discover new ideas about origami. Ideas like the axioms of origami (shown on the next page) have emerged from this conference. These axioms have been used in the programming of origami software, which in turn is used to make new origami designs.

While artists and designers of origami have been doing mathematics with paper, this has hardly been their primary concern – it's a means to an end. For the science of origami, however, understanding the underlying mathematics is the end in itself. This highlights the divide between creativity and logical thinking. Many of the cleverest people around today can do one or the other very well, but not both. The landmark exception to this was Leonardo Da Vinci, who was an inventor, engineer, mathematician, designer, visionary, proportionalist, naturalist and celebrated artist.

Origamists are naturally inclined towards the problem-solving aspect of folding a new model. Some regard each new diagram as a challenge to their dexterity and intelligence; others take a more sculptural and perfectionist approach. The art of origami is not only in the problem solving and mathematics, it is in subtle expression, such as the ability to capture the movement of a gazelle leaping across a field or the the layered wrinkles in the face of a gorilla. Respected origamist Jun Maekawa, discussing the works of Hideo Komatsu, whose geometric style of origami is extremely refined, once commented that that there was very little Yoshizawa in them. He was referring to the intuitive use of paper folding, and especially the use of creative curving or sculpting of paper, as Komatsu's works are very precise.

1

Given two points p1 and p2, there is a unique fold that passes through both of them.

2

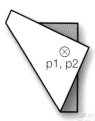

Given two points p1 and p2, there is a unique fold that places p1 onto p2.

3

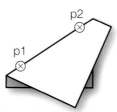

Given two lines L1 and L2, there is a fold that places L1 onto L2.

4

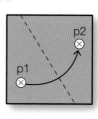

Given a point p1 and a line L1, there is a unique fold perpendicular to L1 that passes through point p1.

5

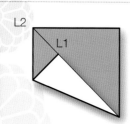

Given two points p1 and p2 and a line L1, there is a fold that places p1 onto L1 and passes through p2.

6

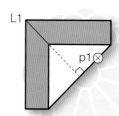

Given two points p1 and p2 and two lines L1 and L2, there is a fold that places p1 onto L1 and p2 onto L2.

7

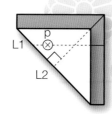

Given one point p and two lines L1 and L2, there is a fold that places p onto L1 and is perpendicular to L2.

The axioms of origami form part of the mathematical foundation of the language of folding. They can be expressed mathematically, or directly with paper. The graphics here show the start and end state of each axiom. Try them out: mark the points and the starting lines, and test out the rules. The result is always a straight-line fold. Robert J. Lang proved that the set is complete for single straight-line folds.

INTRODUCTION
PAPER AND TOOLS

Hideo Komatsu's *Papillon* is a perfect example of his style, rich in geometric proportion and character. Komatsu's models give just the right amount of detail, through shape and colour, for us to recognise a distinct breed of dog.

Anyone who has ever folded a piece designed by Yoshizawa – a master of origami – knows that they must use their intuition and imagination to see where the fold will end up. In fact, the folder should have the entire folding sequence in mind to understand how each fold will affect the next, cascading on and on to the final form. Yoshizawa's masterful touch on the paper is the outcome of a long meditation prior to folding. Yoshizawa's sincerity in his artwork is immediately apparent when viewing his works in a gallery. I have never felt so deeply moved seeing origami works by another artist. The works indeed carry a spirit.

The cerebral approach of mathematics should not overtake the spirit of origami, but rather add to it. Contemporary origami walks this incredibly fine line between mathematical and artistic purity, on the one hand very calculated, and on the other intuitive, abstract and rich in proportions. Perhaps one of origami's most attractive features is that it represents something. It never tries to be too exact – just enough to capture the spirit of the thing, especially in renderings of natural subjects like plants and animals.

COMPUTATIONAL ORIGAMI

Even though the field of computational origami is quite young, the discoveries made to date have been significant. This is an area ripe for exploration by software engineers with applications in folding. The publications of the Origami Science Mathematics and Education conferences are gradually filling with papers from academics who've toiled over hot keyboards to bring the axioms, origami mathematics and design principles into algorithms that can be computed and applied in software. There are several key leaders in this field and the focus of each of them has been origami design. The following is a brief introduction to their software and its functions.

At the time of writing the software is available for free download on the internet – see the references at the end of this chapter for links. You may wish to use your computer to experiment and see how far your inspiration, powered by state-of-the-art origami software, can take you.

The crease pattern and folded model of Robert Lang's *Scorpion varileg, opus 379*. Designed with the help of TreeMaker, and folded in Origamido® paper.

TREEMAKER & REFERENCEFINDER

Robert J. Lang's pioneering efforts gave us design tools like TreeMaker and ReferenceFinder. The background to this software is explained in his book *Origami Design Secrets* – see the references at the end of this chapter. Lang describes the software in the following way: 'TreeMaker is a tool for origami design. Simply put: you draw a stick figure on a square, assigning lengths to each of the sticks in the figure. Through a series of optimizations and calculations, TreeMaker computes a crease pattern in the square that folds up into that stick figure. Or more precisely, it folds into a shape – called a base – whose "shadow" is the given stick figure.' Much of Lang's firsthand knowledge of origami design is used by TreeMaker to create the crease patterns, ready

for you to shape the folds that will breathe life into your subject. In folding the crease pattern, you have two choices: to mark the paper in some way, or to take the purist route and use only folds. The latter option is made easier with ReferenceFinder. Any position on the paper can be located using only folds, and ReferenceFinder gives a folding sequence that is ranked in terms of accuracy and number of folds. This software demonstrates the way software can support the design process to solve those tricky problems that can arise in origami design.

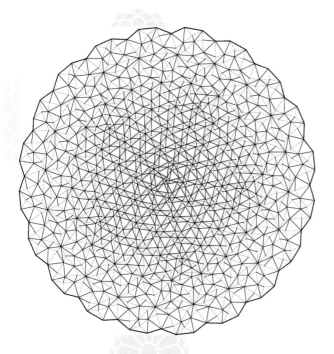

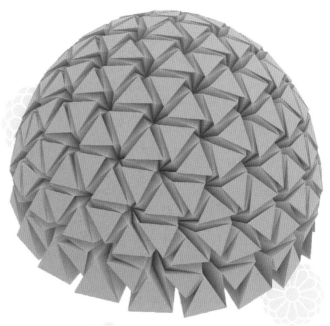

ARCHITECTURAL DESIGN

Tomohiro Tachi is a graduate of Engineering and Architecture at Tokyo University. His innovative software Rigid Origami Simulator, Freeform Origami and Origamizer all have applications for design of folded architecture.

RIGID ORIGAMI SIMULATOR

Rigid Origami Simulator takes the complex problem of understanding and visualising how a given crease pattern will behave kinetically, that is, how all the connected folds will hinge from each other and the form they will create. Not all crease patterns are rigid, and not all are open in a way that means they can move or be simulated, but for those that can – like miura-ori, the Yoshimura pattern or the waterbomb (or ananas pattern) – this tool can show us how they can be formed into three-dimensional structures.

FREEFORM ORIGAMI

Freeform Origami takes a similar approach to Rigid Origami, but adds several elements to the design process. These include rules such as developability (it can be made from a flat sheet), open rigidity (it has some mechanical properties) and the ability to be folded from a square (for origami purists). The software allows the user to manipulate the 3D folded form by dragging the vertices (the points where folds meet) to change the shape. This allows them to create a new aesthetic that matches a given function, and be confident that it can be folded from a flat sheet. Freeform Origami opens up many design opportunities.

Top: Tomohiro Tachi's exquisite Origami Hemisphere crease pattern and computer-generated model, designed and created using his own software and algorithms.

INTRODUCTION
PAPER AND TOOLS

Tomohiro Tachi folds a laser-cut metal sheet into the Stanford Bunny. The crease pattern was calculated by Origamizer.

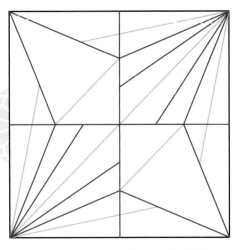

A simple crease pattern drafted with Oripa.

ORIGAMIZER

Origamizer is a tool that takes a 3D model and generates a crease pattern that can be followed to fold the 3D form. The algorithm that does the unfolding is the result of an ongoing collaboration between Tomohiro Tachi and Erik Demaine. Their aim is to prove that the algorithm can unfold any 3D object into a flat crease pattern. The patterns can be incredibly complex and difficult to fold, but Tomohiro Tachi has shown that, with perseverance, they are achievable. His signature model is the Stanford Bunny, a test graphic popular in computer science. The complexity of the patterns highlights the need for machines to simplify the process and for scoring or pre-programming the material with the crease pattern before folding.

ORIPA, ORIGAMI PATTERN EDITOR

When you need to design an origami crease pattern or reconstruct one from an unfolded model, look no further than Oripa, the origami pattern editor designed by computer science professor and origami artist Jun Mitani. Oripa is based on useful origami design principles such as mountain/valley assignment of creases, a variable grid and the direct application of origami axioms as common folding calculations. For example, a few clicks between two lines can divide an angle – an application of axiom three. Oripa can also do a flat-foldability check and shows the flat folded model. Oripa also exports to common CAD formats, making it useful for working with machines and other software. Related software by Mitani includes Pepakura, a commercial tool for converting 3D designs into paper craft (cut, fold and glue process), as well as Twist Origami, a tool for designing models with rotational symmetry.

TECHNO ORIGAMI

Techno origami refers to the use of technology to assist with the folding of very precise origami, taking the complicated fingerwork out of complex origami. To use techno origami, the designer must have the crease pattern. The simple way to find the crease pattern of a known origami model is to fold it, then unfold it; the crease lines left in the paper are the crease pattern. The crease pattern does not include the folds that are not used in the final shape – these can be thought of as construction folds.

Many origamists nowadays use crease-pattern design techniques to design complex origami. They start from the pattern, mapping out the paper with lines and imagining the folded form. Techno origami enables origamists to take a crease pattern design and engrave, etch or mark the pattern into the paper, speeding up prototyping and increasing the accuracy of the final form. It should be noted that techno origami is destructive: a laser or knife cuts into the paper and this damage is much more extensive than the damage caused by pure folding. There are alternatives to cutting, described in the Decoration chapter. The following pages give a simple overview of techno origami.

A folded wall produced from cardboard on an industrial flatbed cutter and folded by hand. The design was made in modular pieces, with cuts and folds to minimise use of material, then glued and mounted onto a specially built wooden frame, designed to complement the aesthetic of the Oribots.

In the shadows of this unfolded sheet, we can see the crease pattern of mountain and valley folds.

A crease pattern drafted in computer software. The choice of cutting tool, software and technique can allow for different line colours to be cut on different sides of the paper and at different power settings. Colour is used to distinguish between mountains, valleys and the edge of the paper.

DESIGN

There are two basic phases for design. The first is design of the pattern itself (this is not detailed here). The second is to put it into a machine-readable format. This is done using CAD, or Computer Aided Design. The design tells the machine where to make marks on the sheet. It is a combination of lines or curves that are exactly positioned in the digital drawing. Many origami designers are quite adept at using software for their designs. Commercial and open-source software is readily available, such as Adobe Illustrator, Inkscape, CorelDRAW and Oripa.

MARK

The aim of techno origami is to mark the crease pattern by making a slight cut into the surface of the paper without going all the way through. In the printing industry this is done by roll or stamping machines with special dies. The cost of setting up a die is expensive, and for a one-off, complex origami base, no one would bother. But with a laser, any computer drawing can be etched onto a sheet of paper, and quickly. In techno origami we use special tools such as hobby cutters, laser cutters and industrial flatbed cutters.

A fold being made in laser-scored elephant hide paper. The white lines are the marks made by the laser. A gentle bend is all that is needed to start the fold.

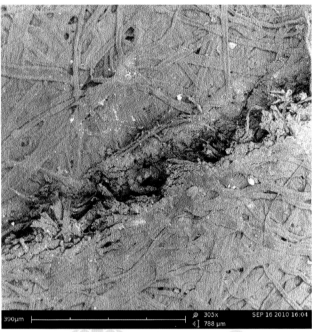

A laser-cut score in elephant hide paper, magnified 305, looks like a gash in the paper. Practically, it is a fold-guiding luxury, saving hours of work in pre-creasing complex patterns.

FOLDING

Folding using techno origami is just like normal origami, but because the paper is pre-programmed, the folding process is much quicker, highly accurate and reproducible. The main difference is that the cut in the paper guides the fold very accurately, and the folder only needs to slightly bend the paper and the fold line will begin to appear. It really is a pleasure to fold paper using techno origami.

MACHINES FOR MARKING FOLDS

Many different machines can be used for marking folds. The tools mentioned on the next two pages are listed roughly in order of expense. They all require expertise and experience to operate. You might get access to one of these machines at a university or at a fab lab (fabrication laboratory) in your city. Take some time to learn how to use the machine first, then do lots of small trial cuts and folds to get it working nicely with your chosen paper stock. The best results fold easily but don't damage the paper too much.

INTRODUCTION
TECHNO ORIGAMI

Jeffrey Rutzky used his Craft ROBO to cut and score this georgeous *Polar Light* by artist Chris K. Palmer.

HOBBY CUTTERS

The series of home-computer-controlled cutters from Graphtec is useful for small projects (the Craft ROBO Pro is good for up to A3 size), light card and some thin plastics such as polypropylene. The machines are similar to small plotters like those used in the vinyl sign industry. Graphtec realised that a computer-literate public would be quick to take advantage of this kind of machine. Jeffrey Rutzky, a New York designer, took the art of using the Craft ROBO to unprecedented levels – he's figured out methods for cutting and scoring on both sides of the media. Rutzky has taken the Craft ROBO to places origami hadn't seen before, experimenting with a range of materials and processes. When using the machine, it is important to get the settings right, particularly pressure – how hard the knife is pushed into the paper – and cutting depth. The depth of the cut can be adjusted for various thicknesses of materials. Too deep and you will cut all the way through; too shallow and the cut won't have any effect.

These colourful 14-side tatos by designer Philip Chapman-Bell were made by Jeffrey Rutzky using his Craft ROBO.

LASER CUTTER

A laser cutter normally has a flat cutting area over which the laser moves, and the material cut by a laser is usually a flat uniform height. You need access to a low-power laser for paper – around 30–100 watts. Too much above that level and instead of making a slight score in the paper, you'll end up blasting a hole all the way through. We have been using a Trotec Rayjet, which has three main settings. Focus refers to the height of the laser above the material. This is set by the height of the material – for paper it's usually a fraction of a millimetre. Speed control affects how quickly the laser moves across the material while cutting: slow means more energy but higher accuracy, and fast uses less energy but provides less accuracy. Power controls the strength of the laser – full power on the Rayjet can only just cut through 3mm (1/8 inch) of acrylic plastic. The settings used really depend on the laser and the material. If you have plenty of time to make your project, then I suggest a slower speed and lower power, for the sake of the quality of your work.

INDUSTRIAL FLATBED CUTTER

Large flatbed knife cutters are wonderful tools, but very expensive, and are usually owned by a company rather than an individual. The process is very particular to the machine – again, speed, pressure/power and the choice of knife are very important. The machines I have seen all have a vacuum bed, which holds the material in place while cutting. The knives can be changed to scoring tool heads, and the pressure and speed are far superior to hobby cutters like the Craft ROBO. The best option is to find a company in your local area – they are usually involved in packaging and use the machine for making prototypes. Find out what file format they use and which materials they can cut and score.

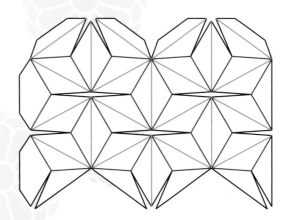

The crease pattern design for the folded wall shown on page 23. The black outline is cut, the red lines are the mountain folds, and the blue the valley folds.

ORIGAMI SYMBOLS

LINES

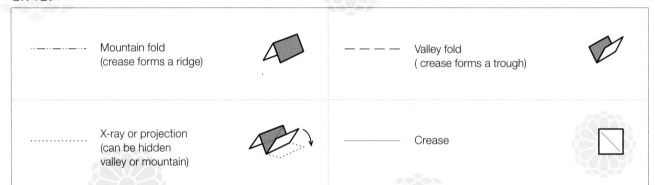

– · – · – ·	Mountain fold (crease forms a ridge)	– – – – –	Valley fold (crease forms a trough)
· · · · · · · ·	X-ray or projection (can be hidden valley or mountain)	———	Crease

ARROWS

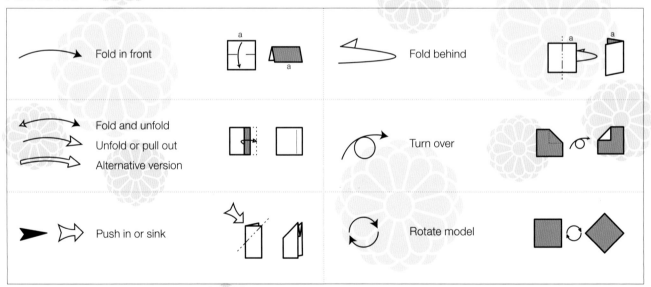

	Fold in front		Fold behind
	Fold and unfold / Unfold or pull out / Alternative version		Turn over
	Push in or sink		Rotate model

EXTRAS

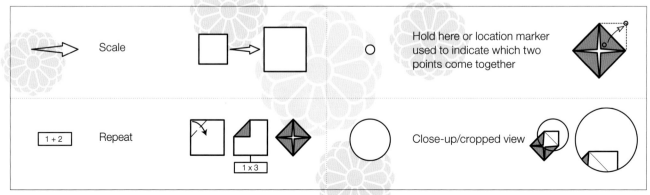

	Scale	O	Hold here or location marker used to indicate which two points come together
1 + 2	Repeat		Close-up/cropped view

TYPES OF FOLDS

BOOK FOLD

Valley fold one edge to another, like closing a book.

CUPBOARD FOLD

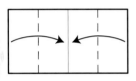

Fold both edges to the middle crease, like closing two cupboard doors.

BLINTZ

Fold all corners to the middle. Named after a style of pastry called a blintz.

PLEAT

A mountain and valley fold combination.

BISECT
Divide a point in two

Many folds use a corner and two edges to position the fold line. The most common is a bisection, or division of an angle in two.

Fold one edge to meet the other, making sure the crease goes through the corner.

INSIDE REVERSE FOLD

The spine of the existing fold is reversed and pushed inside.

OUTSIDE REVERSE FOLD

The spine of the existing fold is reversed and wrapped outside.

DOUBLE REVERSE FOLD

A double reverse fold is two reverse folds made in sequence on the same point.

The last diagram shows the paper slightly unfolded, to illustrate the folds that are made.

INSIDE CRIMP   OUTSIDE CRIMP

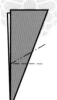    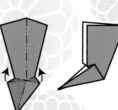

Crimps are often used for making feet or shaping legs. They can be thought of as a pleat mirrored on both sides of the point.

An inside crimp tucks the pleat on the inside of the point.

An outside crimp wraps the pleat over the outside of the point.

PETAL FOLD

The petal fold is found in the bird base.

1

Fold top layer to the centre crease.

2

Fold and unfold the top triangle down. Unfold flaps.

3

Lift the top layer upwards.

4

Step 3 in progress; the model is 3D. Fold the top layer inwards on existing creases.

5

Completed petal fold.

SQUASH

A squash fold is the symmetrical flattening of a point. The flattening movement is known as squashing the point.

1

Pre-crease on the line for the squash fold.

2

Open up the paper by inserting your finger. Fold the paper across.

3

As you put the paper in place, gently squash the point into a symmetrical shape.

4

Completed squash fold.

OPEN SINK

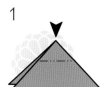

1

Pre-crease through all layers along the sink line. It's best to make a mountain and a valley fold on this line.

2

Open out the point, and push the point into the paper. Take care to reverse folds as shown.

3

The sink should squash flat. Completed sink.

CLOSED SINK

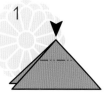

1

A closed sink is the same as an open sink, except there is no possibility to open up the point.

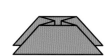

2

Simply push in the point as neatly as you can manage. It takes lots of practice.

RABBIT EAR
The rabbit ear fold is named after its most useful shape – that of a rabbit's ear. It is used to make a new point.

1	2	3	4	5	6

1–3. Divide each corner of the triangle with valley folds.

Fold top edges to the bottom. The middle crease will form a point.

Fold the point to one side.

Completed rabbit ear.

DOUBLE/3D RABBIT EAR
The double rabbit ear is a rabbit ear fold that is mirrored on both sides of the point.

1	2	3	4	5	6
	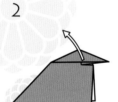	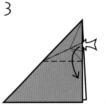			

Make a rabbit ear fold on the point.

Unfold the rabbit ear.

Squash fold the point.

Inside reverse fold the two points.

Valley fold the point upwards.

Completed double rabbit ear.

SWIVEL FOLD

1	2	3

A swivel fold is often made on a pleat. It narrows its two points, and the excess paper swivels under one of the points.

ORIGAMI BASES

WATERBOMB BASE

1

2

3
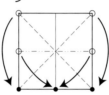

4

Begin coloured side up. Book fold and unfold.

Turn over, fold and unfold diagonals.

Collapse on existing creases.

Completed waterbomb base.

PRELIMINARY BASE

1
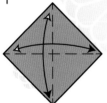

2
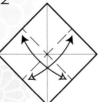

3
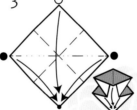

4

Start coloured side up. Fold and unfold diagonals.

Turn over, book fold and unfold.

Fold the side corners, followed by the top corner, to meet at the bottom corner.

Completed preliminary base.

BIRD BASE

1

2

3
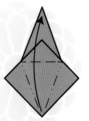

4

Start from the preliminary base. Make a petal fold (see page 29). Turn over.

Petal fold completed. Turn over.

Make another petal fold.

Completed bird base.

REFERENCES

SELECTED BOOKS

Origami Design Secrets: Mathematical Methods for an Ancient Art. Robert J. Lang, Taylor and Francis, 2011.

Shadowfolds: Surprisingly Easy-to-Make Geometric Designs in Fabric. Jeffrey Rutzky and Chris. K. Palmer, Kodansha USA, 2011.

Origami Tessellations: Awe-Inspiring Geometric Designs. Eric Gjerde, A. K. Peters, 2008.

Folding Techniques for Designers: From Sheet to Form. Paul Jackson, Laurence King Publishers, 2011.

Everything Origami. Matthew Gardiner, Hinkler Books Pty Limited, 2008.

International Meetings of Origami Science, Mathematics and Education:
Origami[3]. editor T. Hull, A. K. Peters, 2002.
Origami[4]. editor R. J. Lang and OrigamiUSA, A. K. Peters, 2009.
Origami[5]. editor P. Wang-Iverson, R. J. Lang and M. Yim, A. K. Peters, 2009.

ARTISTS / PROGRAMMERS

Robert J. Lang www.langorigami.com
Jun Mitani mitani.cs.tsukuba.ac.jp
Tomohiro Tachi www.tsg.ne.jp/TT/origami/

ARTISTS / DESIGNERS

Eric Joisel www.ericjoisel.com
Satoshi Kamiya www.folders.jp
Chris K. Palmer www.shadowfolds.com
Joseph Wu www.origami.as
Makoto Yamaguchi www.origamihouse.jp

SOCIETIES

Assoc. Española de Papiroflexia www.pajarita.org
Australian Origami www.papercrane.org
British Origami Society www.britishorigami.info
Danish Origami Society www.foldning.dk
Centro Diffusione Origami www.origami-cdo.it
Hungarian Origami Society www.ori-gami.hu
Japan Origami Academic Society www.origami.gr.jp
Mouvement Francais Plieurs Papier www.mfpp-origami.fr
Nippon Origami Association www.origami-noa.com
Origami Bolivia www.origamibolivia.tk
Origami Deutschland www.papierfalten.de
Origami Sociëteit Nederland www.origami-osn.nl
OrigamiUSA www.origamiusa.org
The Israeli Origami Center www.origami.co.il

ORIGAMI JEWELLERY

Making origami jewellery is a fun and creative way to make use of the distinctive colour and patterning of origami paper. This section will guide you through a range of earrings, brooches and bands. You will need jewellery hardware, beautiful papers and protective coatings to complete these projects.

Most craft stores carry a range of jewellery hardware for hobbyists. Brooch pins and earrings come in many varieties. Here we recommend a few simple, inexpensive types for getting started. As you gain experience you may want to experiment with more elaborate arrangements and hardware.

EARRINGS

The illustration to the right shows the style of earring used in this chapter, with a hook for the earlobe and a loop at the bottom so you can attach your origami creation.

BEADS

Beads are used to secure the origami at the bottom of the thread. Choose bead colours that are complementary to your paper or jewellery hardware.

BROOCH PINS

Brooch pins have a simple clasping pin, and a flat surface for fixing the pin to the origami model.

GLUE

Hot glue is great for quickly attaching hardware such as brooch pins, as it sets very quickly. For paper to paper, craft glue and PVA (Polyvinyl Acrylate) glue both work well and dry clear.

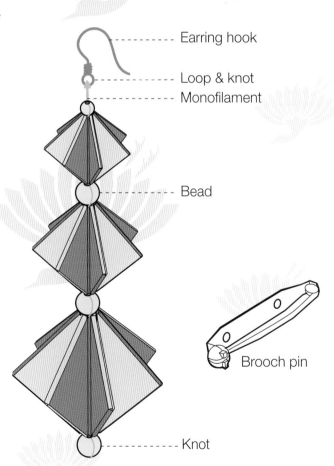

Earring hook
Loop & knot
Monofilament
Bead
Brooch pin
Knot

MONOFILAMENT

Clear nylon thread, also known as fishing line, is used to thread the beads and the origami model, then tied to the jewellery hardware. A clinch knot is used to tie the monofilament – see page 5 of this section for instructions.

BEAUTIFUL PAPERS

Along with the papers supplied with this book, we highly recommend a trip to your local craft store, to investigate the range of patterned papers. By far the most beautiful paper in the world is handmade Japanese washi paper, and chiyogami, but there is an enormous range of beautiful papers to choose from for your origami jewellery project.

PROTECTIVE COATING

Paper is fragile and can be damaged by water and handling. The best way to protect your origami jewellery is to apply a protective coating.

We recommend two simple coatings:
1. Quick-drying clear nail varnish.
2. Clear lacquer in a spray can.
Both methods will harden the paper and also protect it from light moisture. The easiest method is to carefully paint the finished model with nail varnish.

TIPS FOR APPLYING PROTECTIVE COATING

Don't saturate the model with varnish or lacquer – this will soften the model, changing its shape. Instead, use light coats, applying a new coat after the previous one is completely dry. Practise coating a sample of paper before starting on your folded model. We recommend water-soluble lacquers such as polyurethane, or other sprays that are eco-friendly and non-toxic. Read the safety instructions, and apply the coating in a well-ventilated room.

TEARDROP EARRINGS

The simple but elegant shape of this teardrop hangs nicely as an earring, facing either up or down. The final stage shows how to mount the earrings onto jewellery hardware.

SHEET SIZE: 90 X 90MM (3.54 X 3.54IN)
FINISHED SIZE: 65 X 45MM (2.55 X 1.77IN)
MODEL: EVI BINZINGER
DIAGRAM: EVI BINZINGER

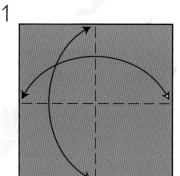

1

Book fold horizontally and vertically, then turn over.

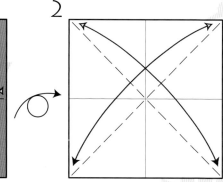

2

Crease both diagonals.

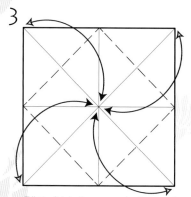

3

Blintz fold all corners to the centre, then unfold.

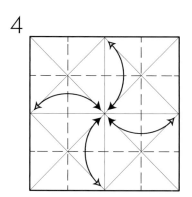

4

Fold and unfold each edge to the centre crease.

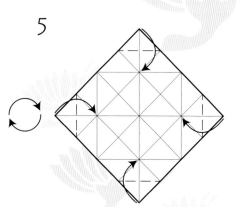

5

Fold each corner in.

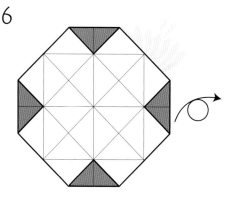

6

The result looks like this.
Turn over.

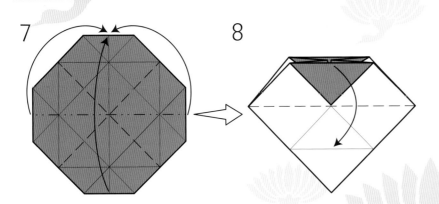

7

Make a preliminary base fold using existing creases.

8

Valley fold the top flap down.

9

Repeat step 8 on the remaining three flaps.

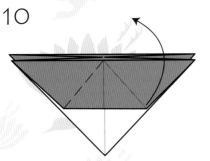

10

Lift up the flap, just enough to complete the next step.

11

Tuck in the point and close the flap again.

12

Lift the point upwards and squash the point.

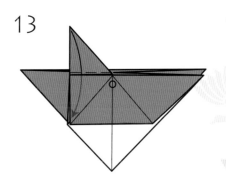

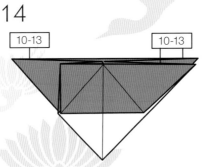

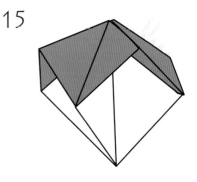

13

Open a little at the marked circle, then tuck the point into the pocket.

14

The lock is completed. Repeat steps 10-13 on the remaining three points.

15

Spread the inner flaps evenly and you will have a finished teardrop.

16

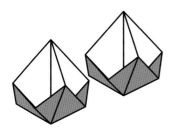

Fold a second teardrop so you can make a pair of earrings.

EARRINGS

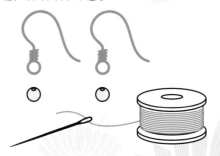

Prepare two beads, two earring hooks, two pieces of monofilament about 15cm (5.9in) and a needle.

2

10cm (3.9in)

Tie each bead onto a piece of monofilament (see knot below). Allow 10cm (3.9in) of extra filament for threading.

3

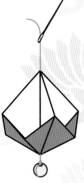

Using the needle, thread the filament through the centre of the teardrop.

4

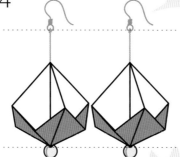

Make sure both teardrops are hanging evenly, then tie each onto a hook (see below).

5

Complete with a protective coating, such as clear nail varnish.

CLINCH KNOT

Make a loop of filament through the loop of the hook or bead.

2

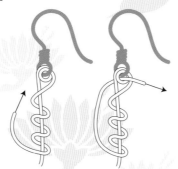

Wrap the filament around itself 3–4 times, then run the end through the first loop.

3

Pull tight and trim the excess.

FAN OF ASIA EARRINGS

Hand fans from Asia are usually made from intricately painted silk or paper. The fans are both decorative and practical. This earring design is inspired by their simple folds.

SHEET SIZE: 90 X 90MM (3.54 X 3.54IN)
FINISHED SIZE: 65 X 45MM (2.55 X 1.77IN)
MODEL: TRADITIONAL, CHINA
DIAGRAM: MATTHEW GARDINER

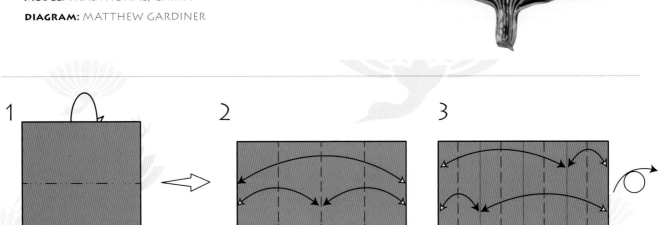

1 Mountain fold in half, so that the colour is on both sides.

2 Fold in half, then 1/4.

3 Fold into 1/8ths. Turn over.

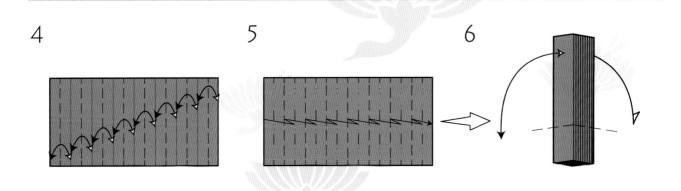

4 Divide into 1/16ths.

5 Pleat on existing creases.

6 Enlarged view. Pinch the bottom quarter together, then fold both ways, through all layers.

7

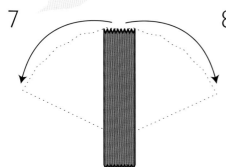

Pinch the bottom, and spread out the upper layers of the fan.

8

Your fan should look like this.

9

Pierce the bottom of the fan with a needle, then bind it tightly with thread and trim.

10

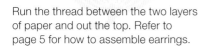

Run the thread between the two layers of paper and out the top. Refer to page 5 for how to assemble earrings.

11

Make a second fan of Asia in order to have a pair of earrings.

12

Complete with a protective coating, such as clear nail varnish. Your fan of Asia earrings are ready to wear.

PUFFY STAR EARRINGS

Τhis traditional model is a symbol for good luck. A string of them make a lovely pendant or set of earrings. We use a strip of paper cut from a regular-sized sheet and fold it into a pentagonal knot.

SHEET SIZE: A4: 21 X 29.7CM (8.26 X 11.69IN)

FINISHED SIZE: 30 X 25MM (1.18 X 0.98IN)

MODEL: TRADITIONAL

DIAGRAM: MATTHEW GARDINER

1

Cut a 1.5cm (0.6in) strip from the sheet of paper.

2

At one end of the strip, make a knot as shown.

3

Gently pull both ends until the pentagonal shape is clearly formed.

4

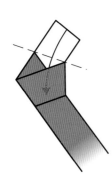

Fold the end of the strip over and tuck under the layer.

5

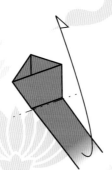

The next steps follow the pentagon shape, wrapping up the puffy star.

6

Valley fold.

7

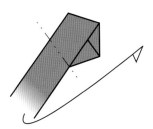

Mountain fold.

8

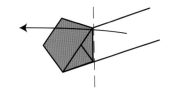

Valley fold.

9

Keep wrapping until you end up with a small stub. Tuck the stub under the next layer.

10

Hold at the circles.

11

Use the back of your fingernail to push in the side of the star.

12

Push in the wall of the star on the remaining sides.

13

Complete with a protective coating, such as clear nail varnish.

14

Make a second puffy star to make a pair of earrings.

15

Refer to page 5 for how to assemble earrings.

PAPER CRANE EARRINGS

The iconic paper crane is a traditional symbol of peace, origami and long life. An ancient Japanese legend says that whoever folds 1000 cranes will be granted a wish. These tiny wishes also make lovely earrings.

SHEET SIZE: 75 X 75MM (2.95 X 2.95IN) OR SMALLER
FINISHED SIZE: 56 X 40MM (2.20 X 1.57IN)
MODEL: TRADITIONAL, JAPAN
DIAGRAM: MATTHEW GARDINER

1

Start with your paper coloured side up. Fold and unfold diagonals. Turn over.

2

Book fold and unfold.

3

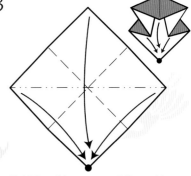

Fold the side corners, followed by the top corner, to meet at the bottom corner.

4

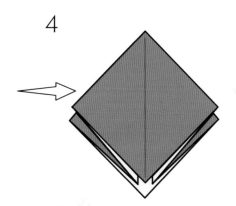

Completed preliminary base.

5

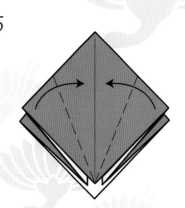

Fold the sides of the top layer to the centre crease.

6

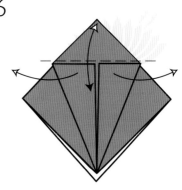

Fold and unfold the top triangle down. Unfold flaps.

7

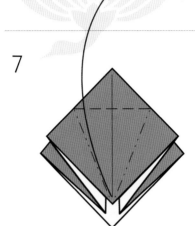

Lift the top layer upwards.

8

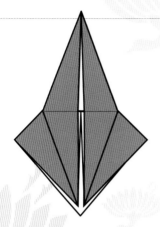

Step 7 in progress: the model is 3D. Fold the top layer inwards on the existing creases.

9

Step 7–8 completed. The model will be flat. Turn over.

10

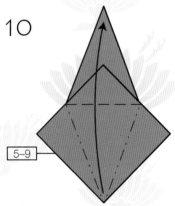

5–9

Repeat steps 5–9 on this side.

11

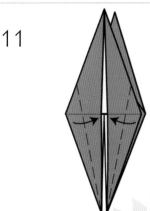

Narrow the bottom points on the top layer only. Repeat behind.

12

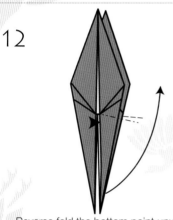

Reverse fold the bottom point upwards.

13

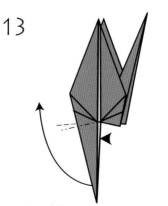

Repeat with the point on the other side.

14

The body is now complete. The next steps focus on the head.

15

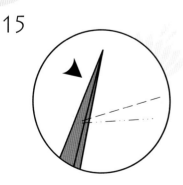

Reverse fold the point to create the head.

16

Head completed.

17

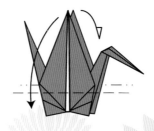

Fold wings down.

18

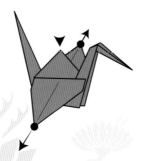

Pull the wings gently to shape the body. The centre becomes rounded.

19

Complete with a protective coating, such as clear nail varnish.

20

Repeat 1000 times for a wish, or just make one more for a pair of earrings!

21

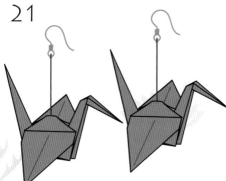

Refer to page 5 for how to assemble earrings.

HEART BROOCH

The heart is a symbol of love and passion. The curved, three-dimensional shape of this heart is ideal for a brooch.

SHEET SIZE: 75 X 75MM (2.95 X 2.95IN)

FINISHED SIZE: 75 X 85MM (2.95 X 3.34IN)

MODEL: EVI BINZINGER

DIAGRAM: EVI BINZINGER

1

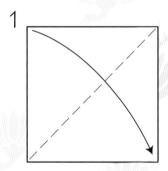

Fold in half diagonally.

2

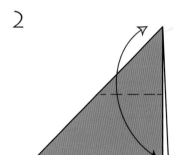

Bring the top point to the bottom corner and crease.

3

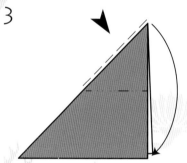

Inside reverse fold the top point.

4

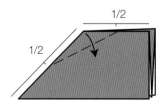

Valley fold, calculating the measurements by eye.

5

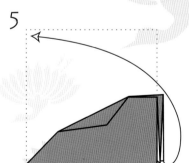

Unfold completely.

6

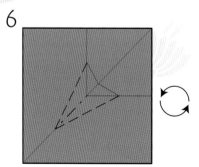

Change the existing crease direction as shown.

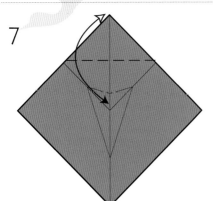

7

Crease the top point.

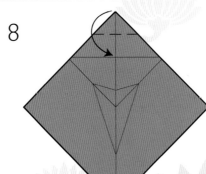

8

Bring the top point to the crease made in step 7.

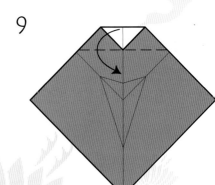

9

Fold along the crease made in step 7.

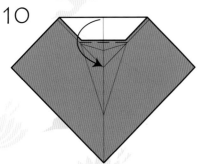

10

Fold along the bottom of the top layer.

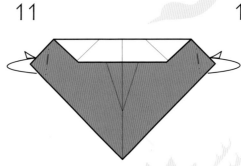

11

Mountain fold the side points behind.

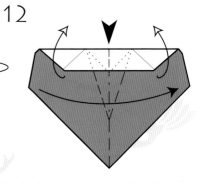

12

Push at centre top, and fold in half, lifting the top layer upwards. Look ahead to steps 13 & 14.

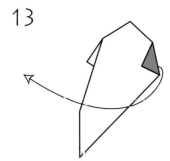

13

The model should now be flat. Unfold to reveal the finished heart.

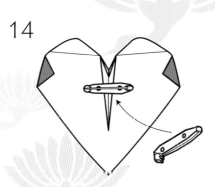

14

Turn over to fix a brooch pin on the back of the heart with glue.

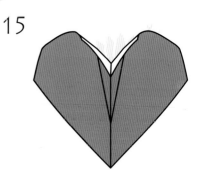

15

The finished heart. Apply a protective coating, such as clear nail varnish.

BUTTERFLY BROOCH

B utterflies capture the imagination of children and adults alike. The abstract shape of this model works best with two-toned paper.

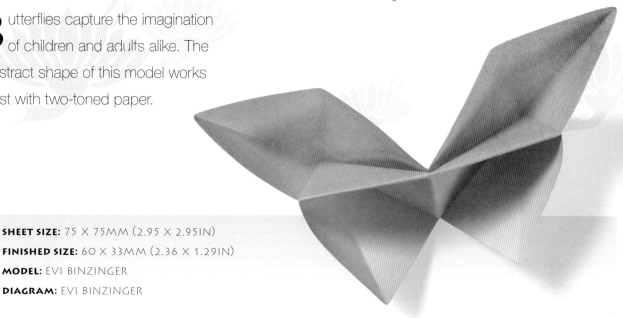

SHEET SIZE: 75 X 75MM (2.95 X 2.95IN)
FINISHED SIZE: 60 X 33MM (2.36 X 1.29IN)
MODEL: EVI BINZINGER
DIAGRAM: EVI BINZINGER

1

Crease one diagonal.

2

Then the other.

3

Fold the top corners to the centre.

4

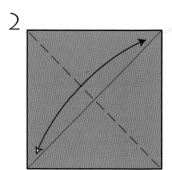

Valley fold and unfold the bottom corners to the centre.

5

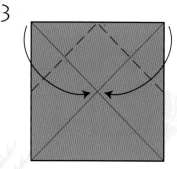

Valley fold bottom edge to the centre. Turn over.

6

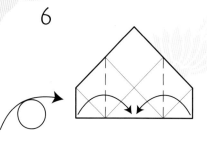

Valley fold edges to the centre.

7

Squash fold points outwards.

8

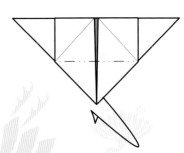

Valley fold at centre.

9

Mountain fold the bottom triangle behind.

10

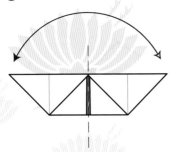

Crease across the centre.

11

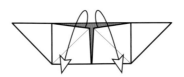

Open out the pockets a little.

12

Open all pockets up.

13

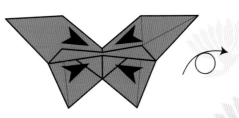

Press the inner points as shown to curve the butterfly's shape. Turn over.

14

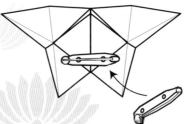

Glue a brooch pin onto the flat section of the bottom wings.

15

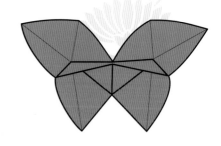

Complete with a protective coating, such as clear nail varnish.

SUMMER EARRINGS

Like radiant summer days, these earrings are beautiful and bright and so simple to make. Use two colours, perhaps one plain and one patterned, for best effect.

SHEET SIZE: 25 X 25CM (9.84 X 9.84IN)
FINISHED SIZE: 10.5 X 3.7CM (4.13 X 1.45IN)
MODEL: MATTHEW GARDINER
DIAGRAM: MATTHEW GARDINER

1
You need two 1/8 strips for each section of one earring. Cut two 1/8 strips from a 25cm (9.84in) sheet.

2
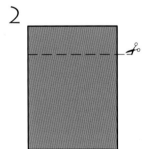
Cut a square from the remaining piece of paper. Measure the sides, and make a fold or pencil mark before cutting.

3
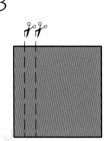
Then cut two 1/8 strips from the square.

4

Cut another square from the remaining paper. Measure the sides, and make a fold or pencil mark before cutting.

5
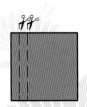
Cut two more 1/8th strips.

6
Now you should have six 1/8 strips of paper in three sizes. You may wish to take the strips from two different coloured sheets for variation.

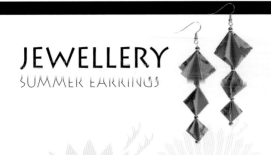

7

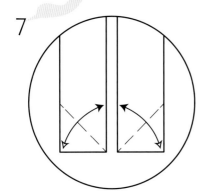

Take two strips of the same length, white-side up, and make a valley fold in the corner of each.

8

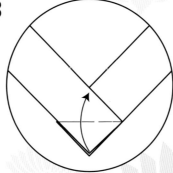

Overlay the two strips as shown, then valley fold through both layers.

9

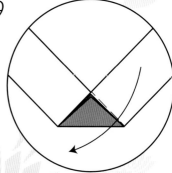

Fold the right side down over the triangle flap.

10

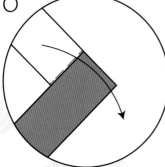

Fold the left side down in the same way.

11

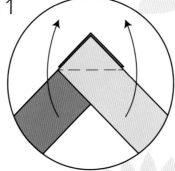

Fold both strips up along the bottom of the triangle.

12

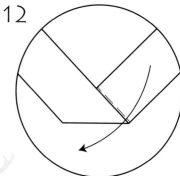

Fold the right side down over the triangle flap.

13

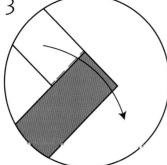

Fold the left side down in the same manner.

14

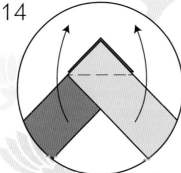

And we are back to the same point as we were in step 11.

15

Repeat steps 8–11 until you reach the end of the paper. There should be seven layers of triangles.

16

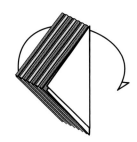

Fold the last triangle around to the front. The triangles will fan out.

17

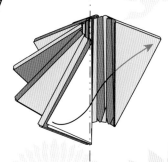

Tuck the two loose flaps into the first pocket as shown.

18

The first section of the earring is now complete. To make the remaining two, repeat steps 7–17.

19

The three sections can be assembled like this.

20

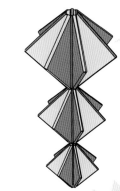

Or like this. Apply a protective coating, such a clear nail varnish, to the finished sections.

21

Refer to page 5 for how to assemble earrings. Thread on a bead between each section.

22

Thread the remaining two modules on, and then tie off onto the earring.

23

Make a second earring to complete the set.

SUMMER ROLL BRACELET

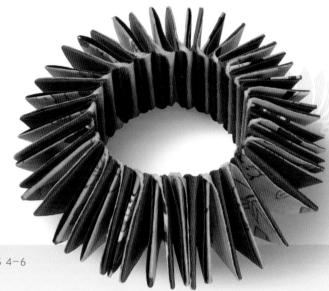

The summer roll is a bracelet of sunshine that can be worn around your wrist. The model has a lock to keep it in place. The long paper is best found on a roll, such as patterned wallpaper.

SHEET SIZE: TWO LONG STRIPS OF PAPER, SEE STEPS 4–6
FINISHED SIZE: SEE STEPS 4–6
MODEL: MATTHEW GARDINER
DIAGRAM: MATTHEW GARDINER

1

Paper on a roll is best for this model, though thin rolls of paper can be hard to find.

2

Wallpaper works well, and comes in a wide variety of colours and patterns.

3

Roll each length of paper out on a flat surface and mark a cut 2.5–5cm (1–2in) from the edge. This will be the width of your bracelet.

4

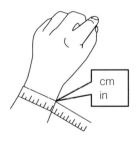

To calculate the length of a paper you will need, first measure the wrist in centimetres or inches.

5

$$\text{Length} = \frac{wrist\ \text{cm}}{0.3} \times paper\ width\ \text{cm}$$

eg.

$$\text{Length} = \frac{21\text{cm}}{0.3} \times 4\text{cm}$$

$$\text{Length} = 70 \times 4\text{cm}$$

$$\text{Length} = 280\text{cm}$$

For metric, divide the the circumference of your wrist by 0.3, then multiply by the paper width.

6

$$\text{Length} = \frac{wrist\ \text{in}}{0.125} \times paper\ width\ \text{in}$$

eg.

$$\text{Length} = \frac{9\text{in}}{0.125} \times 1.5\text{in}$$

$$\text{Length} = 72 \times 1.5\text{in}$$

$$\text{Length} = 108\text{in}$$

For imperial, divide your wrist measurement by 0.125, then multiply by the paper width.

7

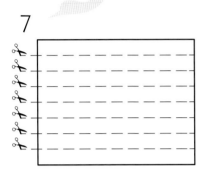

Or divide a large sheet into 1/8s or
1/16s to make long thin strips.

8

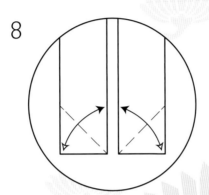

Take two strips, white-side up and
make a valley fold in the corner of each.

9

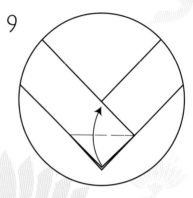

Overlay the two strips as shown, then
valley fold through both layers.

10

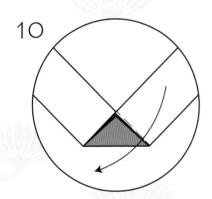

Fold the right side down over the
triangle flap.

11

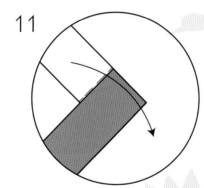

Fold the left side down in the
same way.

12

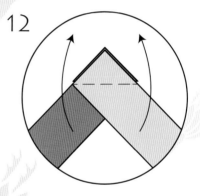

Fold both strips up along the bottom
of the triangle.

13

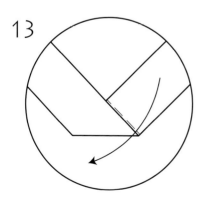

Fold the right side down over the
triangle flap.

14

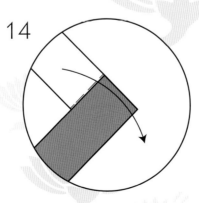

Fold the left side down in the
same manner.

15

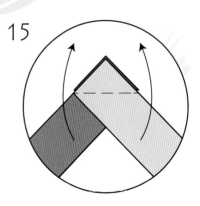

And we are back to the same point as
we were in step 12.

16

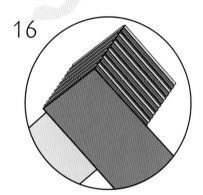

Repeat steps 12–14 and the model will build up as layers of triangles.

17

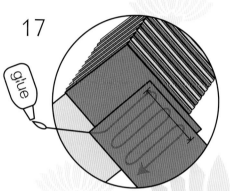

If you run out of paper, glue a new strip on. Allow the width of the paper as overlap.

18

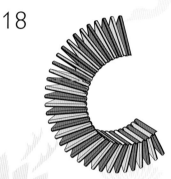

After repeating steps 12–14 several times, the model will become flexible.

19

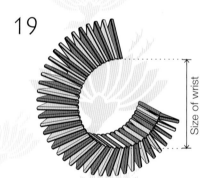

Check the model against the size of your wrist as you work.

20

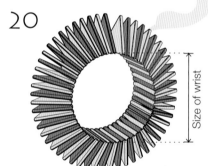

Keep folding until the model wraps around your wrist tightly.

21

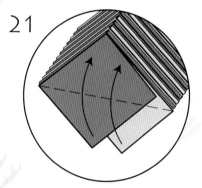

To lock the last triangle, fold the remaining paper up along the bottom of the triangle.

22

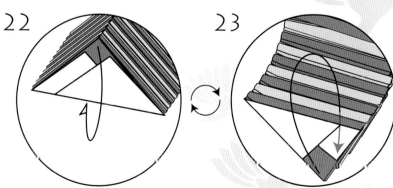

Tuck the last triangle into the previous triangle.

23

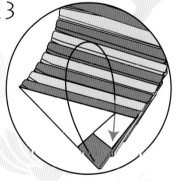

View from the bottom.

24

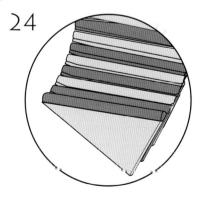

The finished tuck.

25

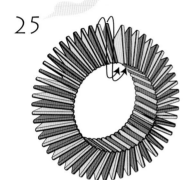

To close the loop, insert two or
more tips into the pockets from the
other end.

26

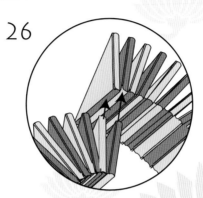

A view from underneath. The points
fit neatly inside the pockets.

27

Apply a protective coating to your
bracelet, or wear it right away,

HEXAGON BROOCH

Designed by Eric Gerde, one of the world's experts in origami tessellations, this relatively simple but captivating design is ideal for a brooch that is beautiful on both sides.

SHEET SIZE: 12.5 X 12.5CM (4.92 X 4.92IN)
FINISHED SIZE: 7.4 X 7.4CM (2.91 X 2.91IN)
MODEL: ERIC GERDE
DIAGRAM: MATTHEW GARDINER

1

Fold in half.

2

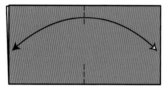

Fold in half horizontally, pinching only at the top and bottom.

3

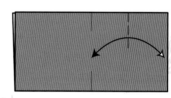

Fold the right edge to the centre, creasing only the top half.

4

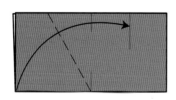

Fold the left corner to meet the crease, pivoting on the centre pinch.

5

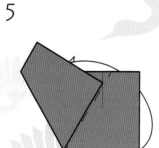

Fold the corner behind, in line with the diagonal edge of the upper layer.

6

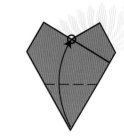

Fold the bottom point up to the intersection of the layers.

7

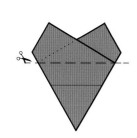

Cut horizontally on a line running through both corners. Unfold the bottom part, turning it white-side up.

8

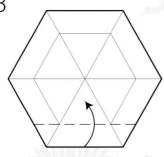

Fold on existing crease, extending to the edges.

9

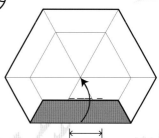

Fold the bottom edge to the centre. Crease between existing crease lines, plus a little extra to the right.

10

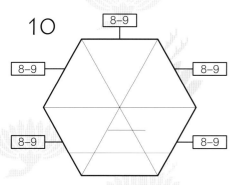

Repeat steps 8–9 on the other five sides.

11

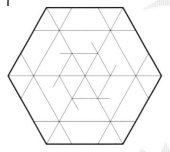

The result should look like this.

12

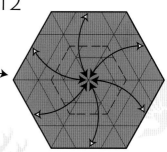

Fold all edges to the centre, taking care to crease between the radial creases.

13

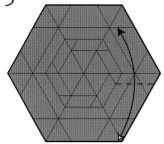

Fold the bottom edge to existing crease. Crease only as shown.

14

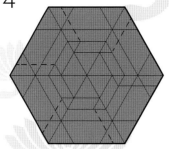

Repeat step 13 on the other five edges (arrows are not shown).

15

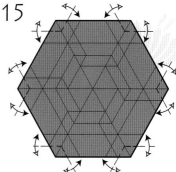

Make short creases on all corners.

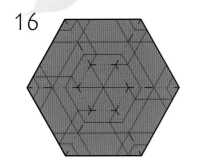

16 Sharpen the mountain folds shown, pinching them a little to give them shape.

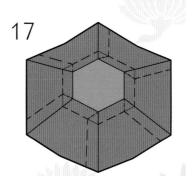

17 Then give shape to the marked valley folds. With these folds shaped it is now possible to begin the collapse.

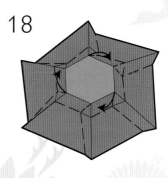

18 Like this. Twisting gently, the valley folds will be gathered underneath the mountain folds.

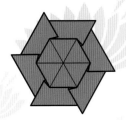

19 It's challenging the first time. This is how it should look from the top.

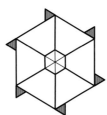

20 And it should look like this from the bottom.

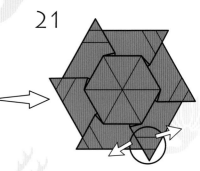

21 The next steps deal with shaping the points. Open up one point a little bit to see the creases.

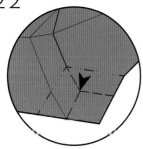

22 Double reverse fold the point on existing creases. Start by indenting as shown.

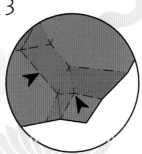

23 Once the pleat is in place, push at the points indicated to collapse it.

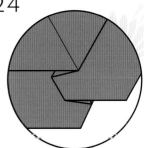

24 It will look like this from the top.

25

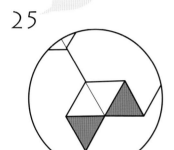

And like this from the bottom.

26

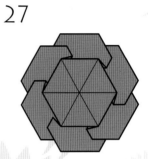

Repeat steps 21–24 on the other five points.

27

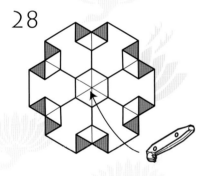

Completed, view from the top. Finish with a protective coating like clear nail varnish.

28

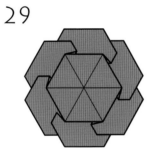

View from the bottom.
Glue a brooch pin to either side – both sides are beautiful.

29

The completed hexagon brooch.

YOSHIBAND

Named after the Yoshimura pattern, this design adds some curves to the idea of a folded armband and could be made larger to form a necklace. The design also features an optional magnetic fastener.

SHEET SIZE: A3: 42 X 29.7CM (16.53 X 11.69IN)

FINISHED SIZE: 2.5CM (1IN) WIDE, RADIUS VARIABLE

MODEL: MATTHEW GARDINER

DIAGRAM: MATTHEW GARDINER

1

Fold in half, then 1/4s.

2

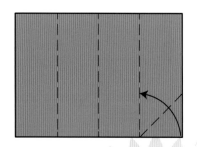

Fold one corner up to meet the first 1/4 crease.

3

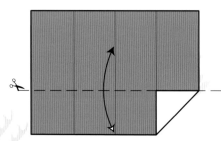

Fold at the top of the triangle, then cut along the crease. A 4x1 sheet is the result.

4

 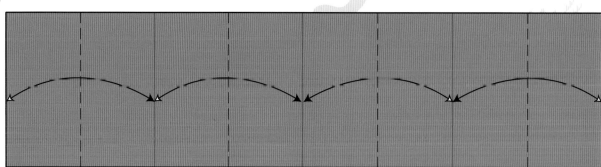

Enlarged view. Divide into 8 across the width.

5

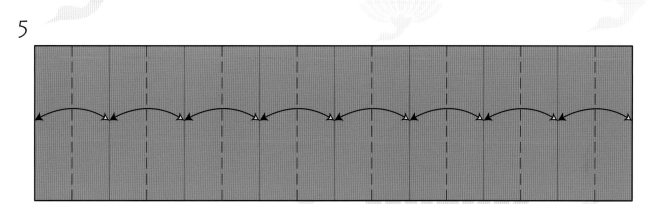

Divide into 16 across the width.

6

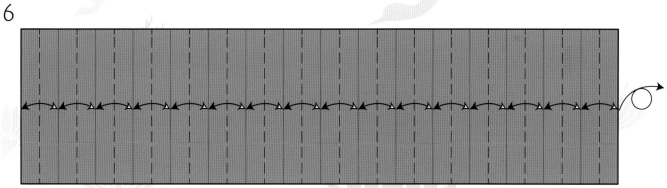

Divide into 32 across the width.

7

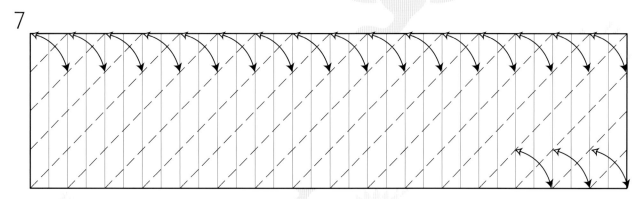

Crease diagonals, using every
second vertical as a guide.

8

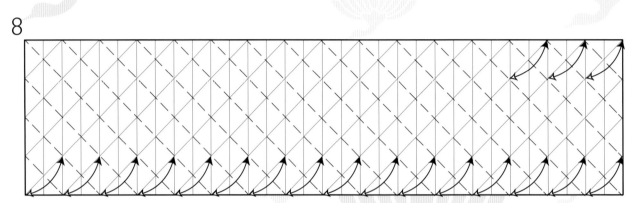

Crease diagonals in the other direction, using
every second vertical as a guide.

9

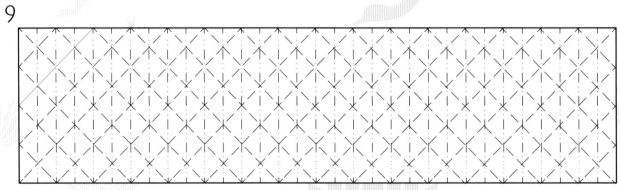

The finished crease pattern, known
as the Yoshimura pattern.

The following steps show how to
collapse the pattern into a tube.

10

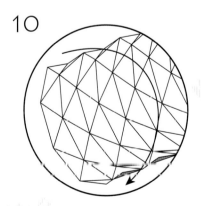

Curve the paper along its length.
Poke the pattern into shape.

11

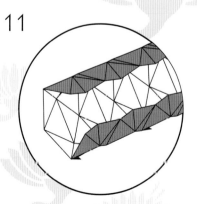

Keep curving. The creases will
become sharper, and the tube tighter.

12

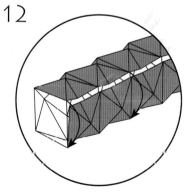

Wrap one edge over the other.

13

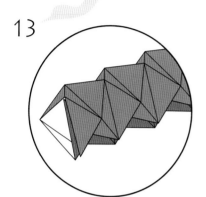

This is close to the final shape.
Now we will check the size.

14

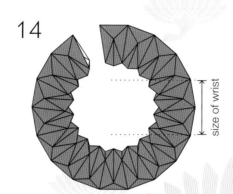

size of wrist

Wrap the model around your wrist, as
neatly as you can without unfolding
the model.

15

overlap   remove

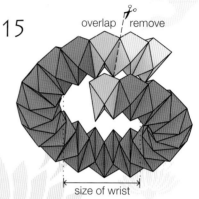

size of wrist

Allow for an overlap of one extra
segment. In this example, cut off two
segments along the valley fold.

16

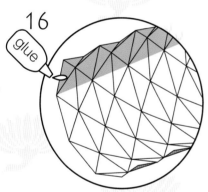

glue

Unfold flat, and apply a light coat of
glue in the grey area shaded above,
along the full length.

17

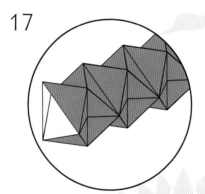

Repeat steps 11–13, then carefully
press the the glued edge into place.

18

5mm
(0.2in)

If you have two small magnets (block,
discs or rings), around 5mm (0.2in) in
size, let the glue dry completely, then
continue from MAGNET CLIP on the
next page.

If you don't have any magnets, then
continue here to make a fixed band.

FIXED BAND

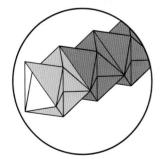

Before the glue dries, open up one
segment at the end. Then set aside
to dry completely.

19A

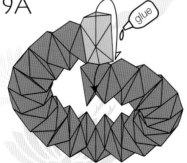

glue

Curve into shape, then wrap the open
segment around the last segment of
the loop and glue into place.

20A

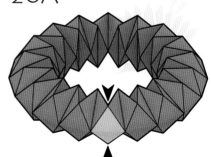

Press each point top and bottom to
curve each outer face.

JEWELLERY
YOSHIBAND

21A

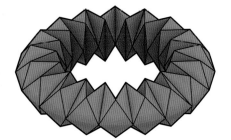

Let the glue dry, apply a protective coating of clear lacquer or nail varnish, and the bracelet is ready.

MAGNET CLIP

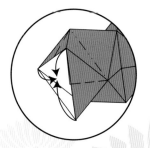

Make sure the glue is dry! At one end, reverse fold the faces in half to form a point.

19B

Magnet

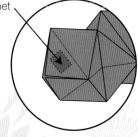

Open up the point and glue one of the magnets on the inside. Glue the point closed.

20B

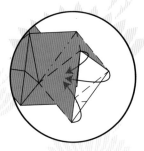

At the other end, fold the faces inwards one at a time, to form an indented point.

21B

Magnet

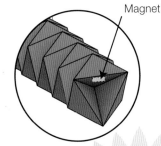

Open up the point. Check that the magnets will attract each other and glue the magnet on the inside.

22B

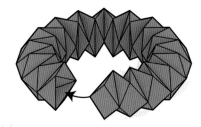

Curve the two points together and the magnets will close the loop.

23B

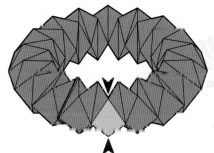

Shape the outer faces, coat with lacquer or nail varnish, and voila!

FOLDS IN FASHION

Origami and fashion have a strong connection. In this section you will learn two techniques that are commonly used in fashion to create folds in fabric: pleating and smocking. Both techniques bring the origami aesthetic into clothing by adding volume, structure, texture and pattern. The origamist will already be familiar with the paper-folding process in pleating, and although smocking seems like it is all about sewing stitches, it actually has a strong relationship to origami designs. First, let's take a look at pleating.

WHAT'S A PLEAT?

The word 'pleat' generally refers to a fold in fabric – usually two alternating folds. Pleats are most often found in skirts, dresses and kilts where they give volume, structure and visual texture. The term has origins in Middle English, a variant of 'plait' – a fold of hair or a braid. There are several ways to put folds into fabrics. The trick is to keep them there, and this will depend on the technique and the type of fabric you are using.

PROFESSIONAL METHOD

Professional pleaters create patterns from two sheets of paper. One pattern can last hundreds of uses. The fabric is compressed between the two sheets and cooked in a steam oven. We will employ a similar method, using a domestic oven with a tray of water. Over the next few pages we will make a simple origami pattern and use it to form permanent creases in a sheet of polyester.

FABRIC FOR PLEATING

It is important to use a suitable fabric for pleating. Polyester, being made from strands of polymer, is ideal because it will permanently deform and hold the folded shape. Use 100% polyester to start with and experiment later with blends. Silks also pleat well, but their creases can soften if warmed to body temperature and pressed. The weave and thickness of the fabric are not so critical but, in general, thinner fabrics will form sharper creases and suit finer and more complex patterns.

Matthew Gardiner's *Oribotics* are made with pleated polyester petals. They are very flexible and deformable. The translucence allows the coloured light to glow through the petals.

PLEATING

PAPER

Most pleaters use a very strong, unbleached brown paper called Kraft paper. The weight of paper to use depends on the complexity of your design. For simple patterns use 150–200 gsm. For complex patterns use 110 gsm elephant hide paper, which is robust and easy to fold. To achieve the best results, you should use two identical patterns. Fold one sheet of paper carefully and patiently, and be prepared to do the same with the second sheet to make it perfect. The patterns are used to produce lots of copies in your fabric, so it's worth the time and effort.

CLAMPS

I use metal clamps, such as bulldog clips, for small projects. Industrial pleaters wrap large patterns in extra layers of paper as well as elastic to keep the fabric compressed during cooking.

Left to right: Kraft paper (commonly known as brown wrapping paper), laser-scored elephant hide paper and folded elephant hide paper.

COOKING

Cook the completed, clamped model in a pre-heated oven at 160°C (320°F) for 15 minutes. Place a tray of water at the bottom of the oven. This will help to prevent the paper from drying out, although the paper will eventually become cracked after many uses.

COOL AND REMOVE

Remove after 15 minutes and leave clamped until completely cool. Carefully unfold the paper and remove the fabric. You now hold a permanently creased sheet of fabric, if this is your first time, congratulations on your first pleat!

PLEATING METHOD SUMMARY

This process can be summed up in five steps:

1. Fold two copies of the origami form into paper.
2. Place fabric between the two sheets of paper (like a sandwich). Align the three sheets carefully and clamp the edges tightly.
3. Collapse all the folds of the 'sandwich' and clamp tightly.
4. Cook at 160°C (320°F) for 15 minutes.
5. Cool, unfold and remove fabric from paper.

ISO-AREA PLEAT

The iso-area twist is a paper-folding technique invented by Toshikazu Kawasaki. It can be used to make pleats in fabric. We recommend that you master this pleating method before making the Ananas Scarf and the M60 Wrap. It is also interesting to compare this technique to the smocking method on page 16.

SHEET SIZE: TWO SHEETS 150 X 150MM (6 X 6IN)
FINISHED SIZE: 75 X 75MM (3 X 3IN)
ISO-AREA TECHNIQUE: TOSHIKAZU KAWASAKI
DIAGRAM: MATTHEW GARDINER

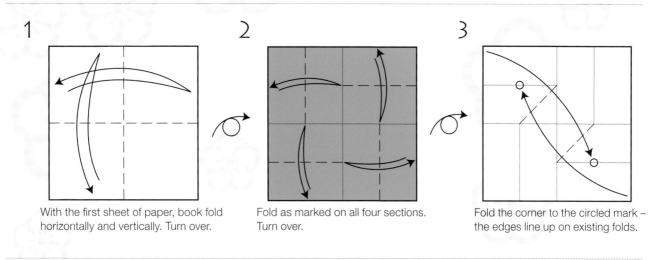

1

With the first sheet of paper, book fold horizontally and vertically. Turn over.

2

Fold as marked on all four sections. Turn over.

3

Fold the corner to the circled mark – the edges line up on existing folds.

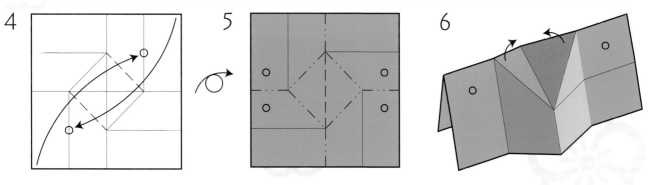

4

Repeat as in step 3.

5

Pre-creasing is done. Pinch at circles and form shape shown in step 6.

6

Push together to form the shape in step 7. No new folds are made.

7

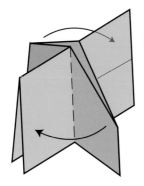

Swivel flaps on opposite sides, and the model will be flat.

8

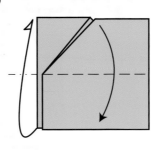

Fold the top front edge down, and the bottom back edge up.

9

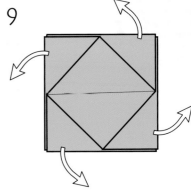

Voila! A simple single iso-area twist. Unfold completely. Repeat steps 1–9 using the second sheet of paper.

10

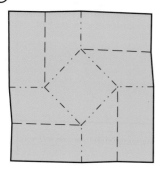

Unfold each sheet. Note the mountain and valley folds.

11

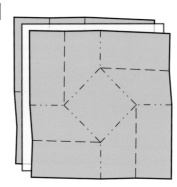

Sandwich the fabric between the two sheets of folded paper.

12

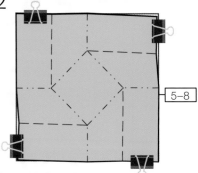

5–8

Align all edges then use small clamps to fix the corners. Collapse all folds – follow steps 5–8.

13

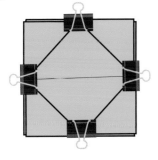

Adjust the clamps to hold all sides firmly, ready for the oven. Refer to cooking directions on page 2.

14

The back of the finished iso-area pleat in the fabric after cooking.

15

The front of the finished iso-area pleat in the fabric after cooking.

ANANAS SCARF

This pleat was named ananas – German for pineapple – because of its many points. With carefully folded paper sheets, you can pleat many beautiful ananas scarves. It takes time, but the result is worth the effort.

SHEET SIZE: 1:4 RATIO, 80 X 20CM (32 X 8IN)
MATERIALS: 2 PAPER SHEETS, POLYESTER FABRIC
FINISHED SIZE: 10 X 50CM (4 X 20IN)
MODEL: MATTHEW GARDINER
DIAGRAM: MATTHEW GARDINER

1

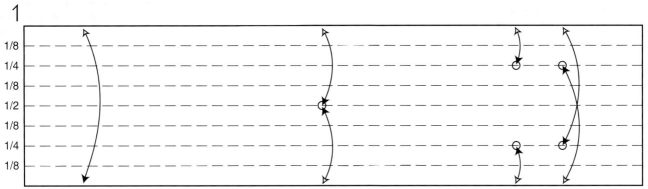

1/8
1/4
1/8
1/2
1/8
1/4
1/8

Begin with a 1:4 ratio sheet. Fold in half lengthways.

Fold at 1/4 marks by folding top and bottom edges to the centre.

Fold at 1/8 marks by folding top and bottom to the nearest crease, and top and bottom to opposite 1/4 crease.

2

1/16 1/8 1/16 1/4 1/16 1/8 1/16 1/2 1/16 1/8 1/16 1/4 1/16 1/8 1/16

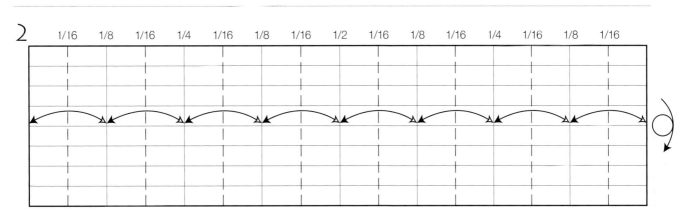

Use the same method as in step 1 to find 1/8ths, folding across the width.

Then divide each 1/8th to get 1/16ths.

Turn over.

3

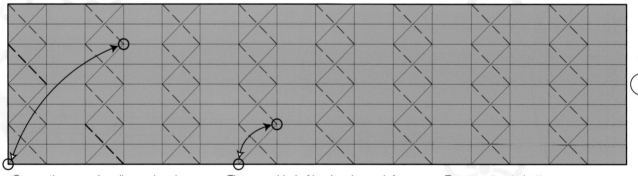

Crease diagonals between folds, skipping every second column. Make marks with pencil if necessary.

All diagonals can be found using existing landmarks.

Note that most landmarks will yield two folds.

4

Crease the opposing diagonals using the same method as in step 3.

The same kind of landmarks work for these folds too.

Turn over top to bottom.

5

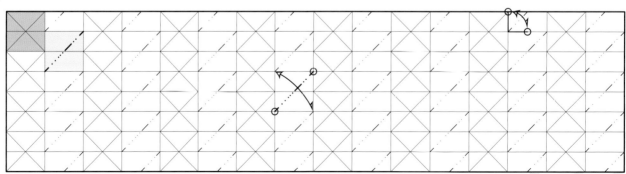

Note that the next set of diagonals are offset by half a square.

Use the intersections of the existing folds as a reference.

Use adjacent corner creases to locate a fold on the edge.

6

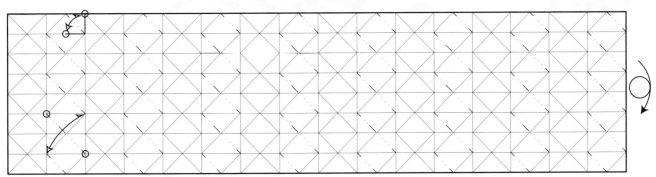

Crease the opposing diagonals using the same method as step 5.

Check ahead to step 7, and make sure your creases are correct.

When you are finished turn over top to bottom.

7

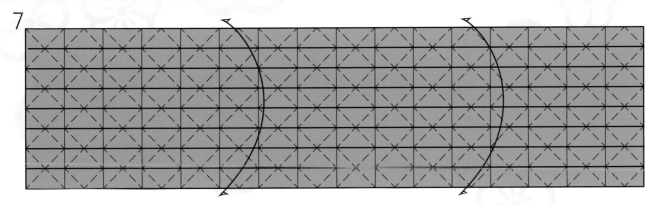

The completed crease pattern. The solid lines show mountain folds, the dashed lines show valley folds.

Begin collapsing the pattern by folding along the lengthwise mountain folds, making the curve you see in step 8.

8

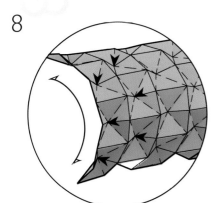

With the paper curved, you can push the creases into shape from above.

9

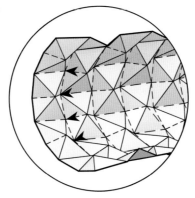

And also from below. Gently 'pop' the creases into place.

10

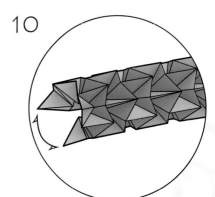

When you get to this stage, it's time to flatten back the other way.

FASHION
ANANAS SCARF

11

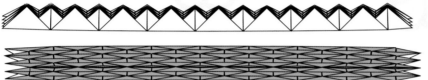

The collapsed pattern from top and bottom. You now need to repeat steps 1–11 using the second sheet of paper.

12

1mm   1mm
1mm
1mm

Prepare a piece of polyester a bit smaller (approx. 1mm (0.04in) on all edges) than the paper.

13

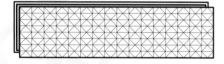

Make a paper, polyester, paper sandwich, then clamp and collapse all three layers. The pleating method is outlined on page 2. Master the iso-area pleat on pages 3–4 before doing the next few steps.

14

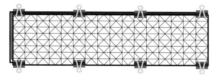

Use small clamps on the edges to hold the fabric in place while collapsing the sandwich. Begin collapsing at one end and work your way along. It takes practice to keep all layers aligned.

15

After collapsing, use big metal clamps to bind the sandwich. Alternatively, you can wrap with string or elastic.

16

After clamping, cook according to the pleating method on page 2.

17

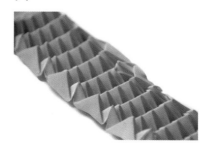

After cooling, remove the clamps. Your result should look like this.

18

The ananas scarf is complete. Wear your work in style.

M60 WRAP

The miura-ori is a folded pattern that has many possible variations. This one has a 60° angle that creates an ordered set of polygons, which looks fantastic as a wrap worn around the neckline or wrist. More than one section can be joined in a loop to make a longer wrap.

SHEET SIZE: A3: 29.7 X 42CM (11.69 X 16.53IN)
STRETCHED SIZE: 29.7 X 42CM (11.69 X 16.53IN)
MODEL: MATTHEW GARDINER
DIAGRAM: MATTHEW GARDINER

1

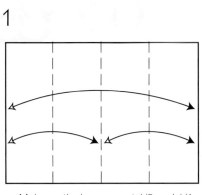

Make vertical creases at 1/2 and 1/4.

2

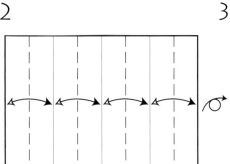

Make creases at 1/8ths.

3

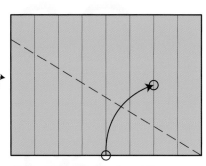

Fold a 30° angle, pivoting at the corner fold so that the edge marked meets the second fold from the right.

4

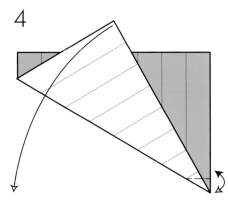

Make a small crease to mark the 1/3.

5

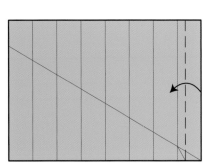

Fold at the 1/3 mark.

6

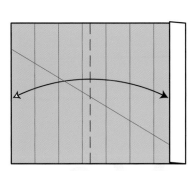

Fold the right edge to meet the inner left edge.

7

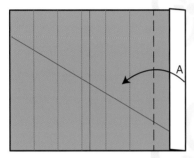

Fold edge A into position by folding on the existing crease.

8

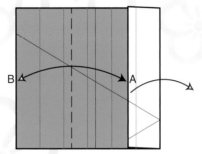

Make a new crease by folding edge B to meet edge A. Unfold.

9

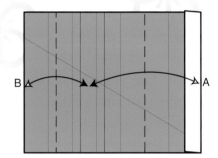

As per steps 7–8, fold edge A, then fold B to meet A. Unfold both.

10

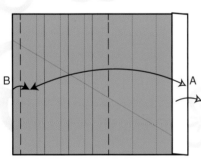

As per steps 7–8, fold edge A, then fold B to meet A. Leave edge B folded, and unfold A completely.

11

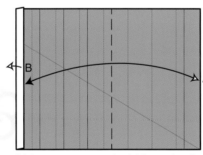

Make a new crease by folding edge A to meet B. Unfold B.

12

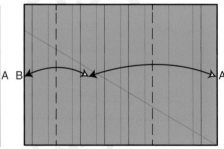

Fold edge B on existing crease, then make a new crease by folding edge A to meet B.

13

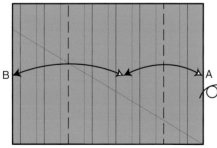

Fold edge B on existing crease, then make a new crease by folding edge A to meet B. Unfold flat. Turn over.

14

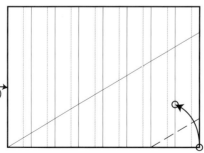

Fold corner to meet first 1/8 crease.

15

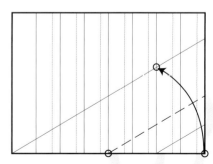

Fold corner to meet second 1/8 crease, and check intersection on bottom edge.

16

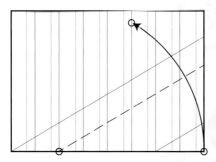

Fold corner to meet third 1/8 crease, and check intersection on bottom edge.

17

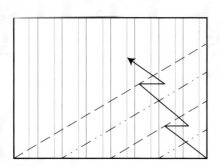

Pleat on existing creases.

18

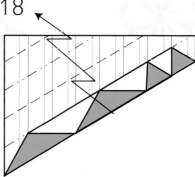

Form new pleats of equal width using the shape of the existing pleats.

19

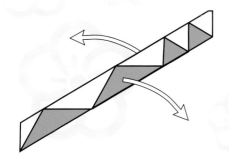

Diagonal pleats completed. Make creases sharp. Unfold.

20

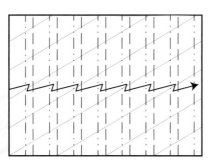

Pleat on vertical creases.

21

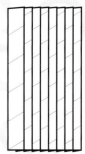

Pleats completed.

22

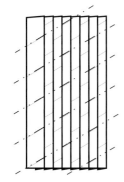

Mountain fold using creases as a guide. Crease sharply through all layers.

23

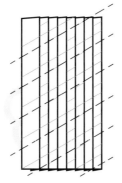

Valley fold using creases as a guide. Crease sharply through all layers.

24

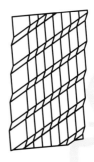

The model will look like this.

25

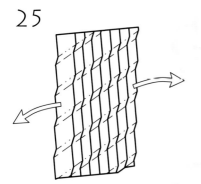

Unfold to a flat sheet.

26

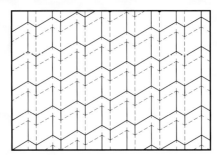

Here we see the creases to use when collapsing. Solid lines show mountain folds, dashed lines are valleys.

27

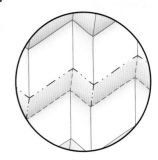

Work along each diagonal pleat from start to finish, gently pushing the pattern into shape.

28

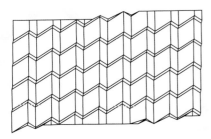

Form all pleats then gently ease the pattern closed.

29

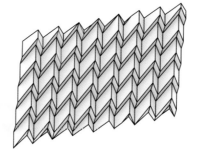

The collapse in progress. Collapse the vertical pleats, from left to right. The diagonal pleats will follow.

30

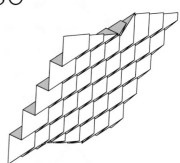

This is the result we seek, and patience will get you there. Now make another one – yes, really!

31

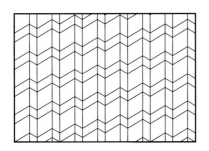

Unfold both sheets as flat as possible.

32

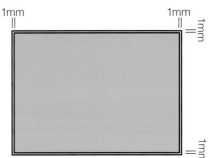

Prepare a piece of polyester smaller (approx 1mm (0.04in) on all edges) than paper.

33

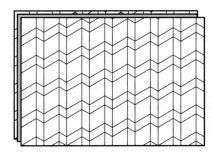

Make a paper, polyester, paper sandwich and follow the pleating method outlined on page 2.

34

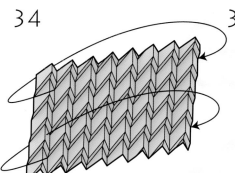

The pleated polyester is very flexible. To make a loop, bring one edge to the other as shown.

35

The light area shows the overlap between the two layers. Clamp or pin before you sew them together.

36

Use a needle and thread to carefully sew along the overlapping inner folds.

37

The finished model is a flexible, stretchable origami form.

38

Use this as a wrist or arm covering, or as a collar. Make it larger, smaller or longer to fit different body parts.

VARIATIONS AND TIPS FOR EXPERIMENTATION

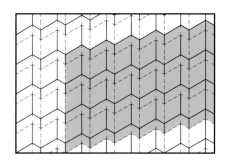

An even pattern (highlighted here in blue) will produce an even loop. You can cut this shape, but remember you also need to cut the polyester to the same shape. Experiment with the following to get new results: change the size and format of the paper, make the fold pattern smaller or larger, and experiment with thicker and thinner polyester fabrics.

SMOCKING

A smocking pattern, 'Taka T2' from page 21, by Takahiro Shirai.

FOLDING FABRIC WITH STITCHES

Smocking is a technique that involves using stitches to put folds and decorative textures into fabric. It's folding without actually folding. Artist Chris K. Palmer introduced smocking to the origami world with his book *Shadowfolds*, in which he uses smocking techniques to create origami-like tessellations. Palmer is inspired by origami master Fujimoto, whose pioneering work revealed the rich complexity of geometry that can be achieved through paper folding. We are going to explore the process of smocking and how it relates to origami. The models are illustrated as t-shirt designs, but they could be applied to any garment.

Smocking is generally done from a pattern. Although the process is quite different to origami, the outcomes are aesthetically very similar. As with the section on pleating, we will start by looking at how to make an iso-twist fold, this time using a smocking technique. But first, let's look at the tools you will need.

TOOLS FOR SMOCKING

1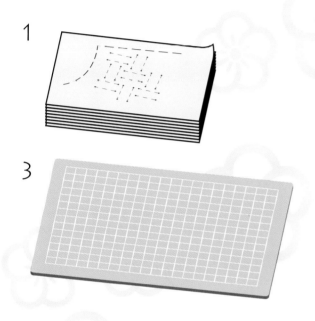

3

2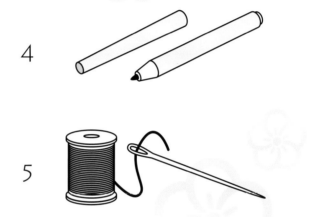

4

5

TOOLS FOR SMOCKING

You will need the following tools for making the templates and sewing.

1. Paper and a photocopier for making copies of the templates. If you don't have access to a photocopier you can use tracing paper to copy the pattern.

2. A 2mm (0.08in) or 3mm (0.12in) hollow punch. This is a thin metal tool with a circular blade at the end. You hold it in position over the fabric, then hit it with a hammer and it cuts out a hole. Hollow punches are available from hardware stores in kits with many sizes.

3. A cutting mat to protect your table when using the hollow punch.

4. Chalk or a washable marker for marking dots on the fabric. Chalk will wash away easily but can also rub off while you are working, so use a washable marker for your first attempts.

5. A needle and thread. It is important to get strong cotton thread, rather than normal thin cotton thread. This is available in sewing or fabric stores.

ISO-AREA SMOCKING

T his is a simple exercise that will demonstrate how smocking relates to origami. We will refold the iso-area twist shown on pages 3–4 of this section, up to step 9. We'll then mark the paper and make it into a smocking template.

SHEET SIZE: 15 X 15CM (6 X 6IN)
MATERIALS: PAPER AND COTTON FABRIC
FINISHED SIZE: 7.5CM X 7.5CM (3 X 3IN)
ISO-AREA TECHNIQUE: TOSHIKAZU KAWASAKI
DIAGRAM: MATTHEW GARDINER

1

Fold steps 1–9 as shown on pages 3–4. Turn over.

2

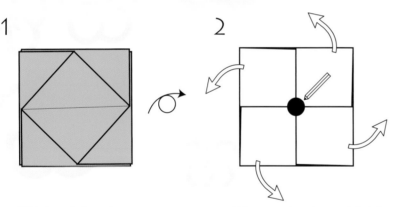

Using a marker, draw a dot at the intersection. Unfold completely.

3

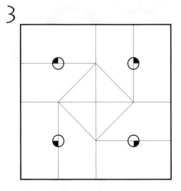

Use a hollow punch to cut four holes at the dots. This is the template.

4

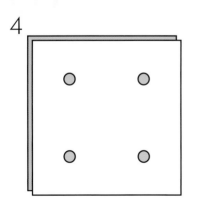

Place the template over the fabric, lining up the corners carefully.

5

Mark the four holes through the paper template onto the fabric. Remove the template.

6

Thread about 15cm (6in) of cotton onto your needle.

7

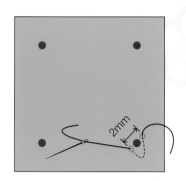

Steps 7–10 show how to make a frontside stich. Make a 2mm (0.08in) stitch under one marked dot.

8

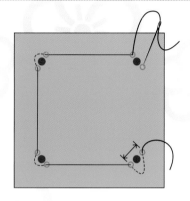

The thread runs over the fabric to the next dot. Make a 2mm (0.08in) stitch under each dot.

9

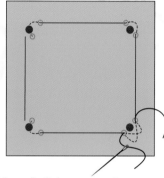

When all stitches are made, prepare to tie a knot.

10

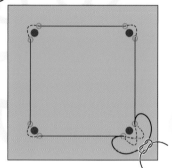

Tie 3–4 overhand knots and pull each one tight. The corners will join up.

11

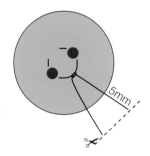

This is a simplified view. Trim the ends of the thread to 5mm (0.2in).

12

It will look something like this – a bit of a mess, but easy to fix.

13

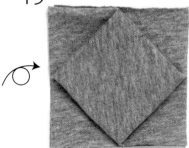

Turn over and press the centre down flat until it forms a diamond.

14

Turn over, then line up the corners of each layer until it looks like this.

15

With a bit of encouragement the folds fall into place. One stitch through four points can do a lot!

TAKA T1

This design by Takahiro Shirai applies origami-style smocking to t-shirts. Many garments, not just t-shirts, can be modified with folds, so experiment and put some origami in your wardrobe!

SHEET SIZE: A4 PAPER FOR TEMPLATE
FINISHED SIZE: N/A
DESIGN: TAKAHIRO SHIRAI
DIAGRAM: MATTHEW GARDINER

1
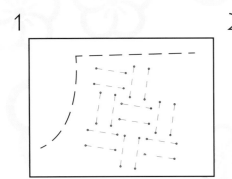
Copy the template on the next page. If you don't have a photocopier, trace it with tracing paper.

2

Cut along the dashed neckline and trim around the pattern. Use a hollow punch to cut out each point on the template.

3
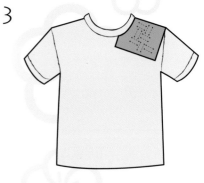
On a flat surface, position the template on an inside-out t-shirt. Align with the top of the sleeve and the collar.

4

Use the template to mark out all the points on the t-shirt.

5

Remove the template and mark the connecting lines for each shape on the t-shirt.

6
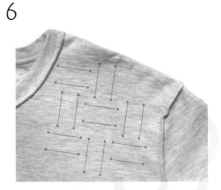
The template has been marked and you are ready to start sewing.

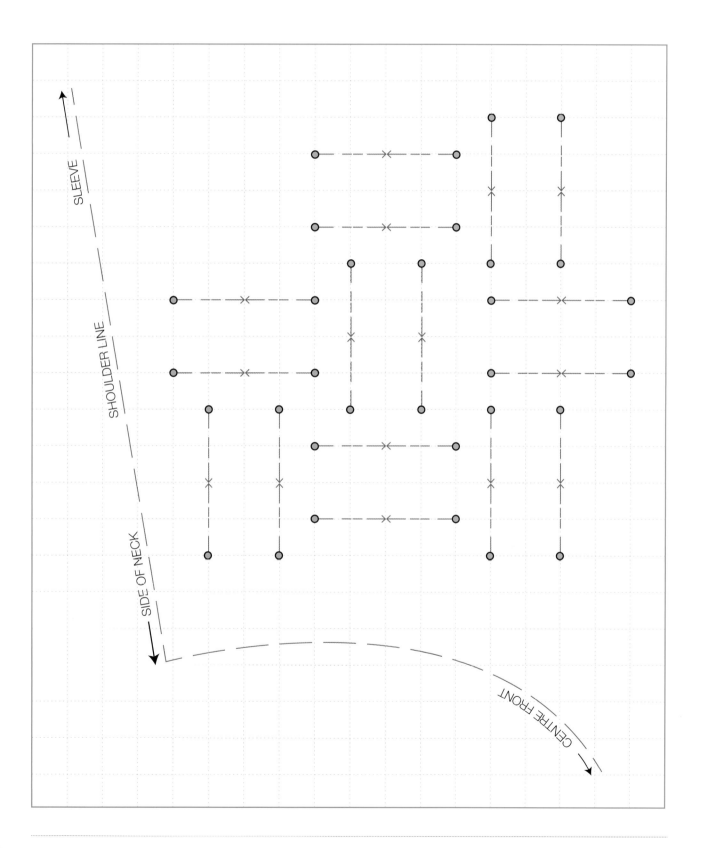

FASHION
TAKA T1

7

Sew a 2mm (0.08in) stitch under the point, then run a frontside stitch between the points.

8

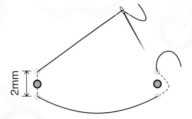

Make a 2mm (0.08in) stitch under the second point.

9

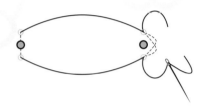

Make another 2mm (0.08in) stitch under the first point so that the thread is on either side of the point.

10

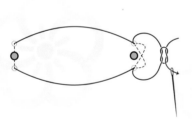

Tie 3–4 overhand knots, pulling each one tight. The two points will join up.

11

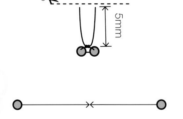

Trim the ends to 3–5mm (0.12–0.2in), then sew the next two points in the pattern.

12

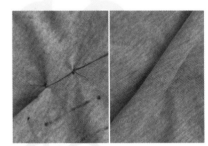

A completed pair of points, inside (left) and outside (right).

13

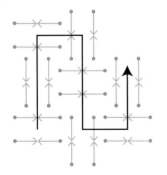

Sew each pattern pair in the order shown.

14

The completed pattern seen from the inside. Trim any loose threads.

15

The completed pattern from the outside. Try it on!

TAKA T2

Takahiro Shirai's second treat for us is a little more complex, featuring a mixture of weaves and windmill-style shapes. The design is intended to be smocked on both shoulders of your garment.

SHEET SIZE: A4 PAPER FOR TEMPLATE
FINISHED SIZE: N/A
DESIGN: TAKAHIRO SHIRAI
DIAGRAM: MATTHEW GARDINER

1

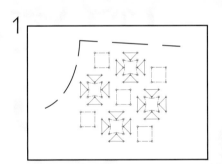

Copy the template on the next page. If you don't have a photocopier, trace it with tracing paper.

2

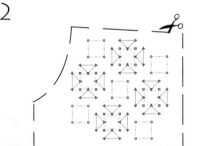

Cut along the dashed neckline and trim around the pattern. Use a hole punch to cut out each point on the template.

3

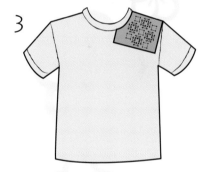

On a flat surface, position the template on an inside-out t-shirt. Align with the top of the sleeve and the collar.

4

Use the template to mark out all the points on the t-shirt.

5

Remove the template and mark the connecting lines for each shape on the t-shirt.

6

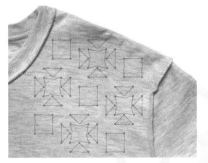

The template has been marked and you are ready to start sewing.

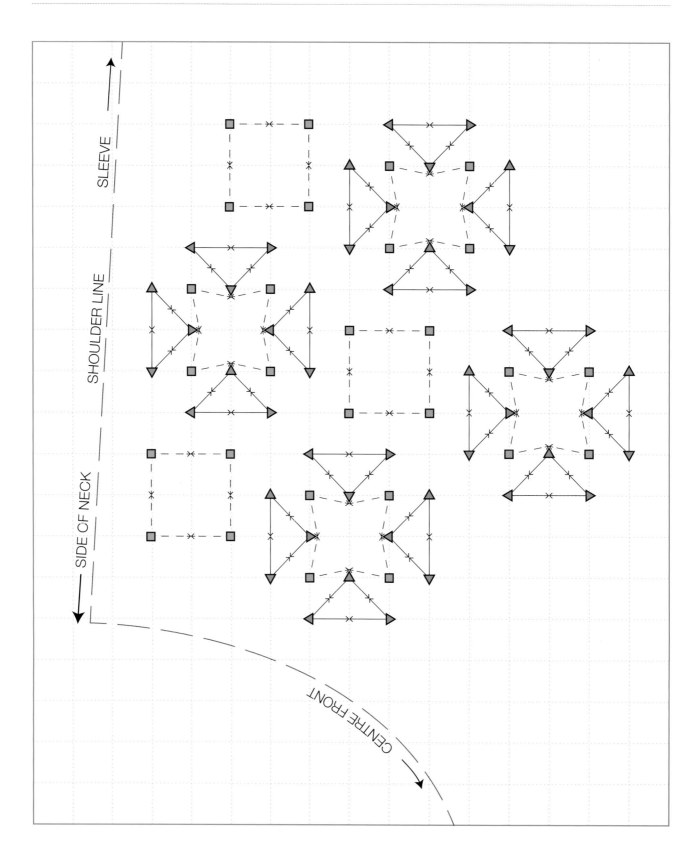

7

Look at the pattern. There are two main pattern types, shown here in yellow and blue.

8

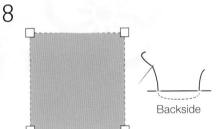

Backside

Start with the squares. The dotted lines in the template indicate a backside stitch. Here's how to do one.

9

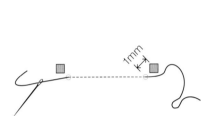

1mm

Start 1mm (0.04in) from a corner and run the thread under, on the backside, to 1mm before the next corner.

10

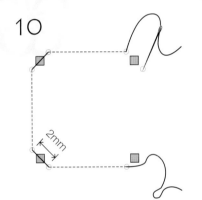

2mm

Sew each corner in order. The stiches are 2mm (0.08in) at the corners.

11

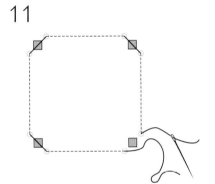

When all the stitches have been made, prepare to tie a knot.

12

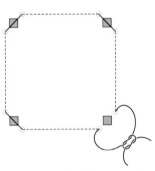

Tie 3–4 overhand knots, pulling each one tight. The corners will join up.

13

5mm

Trim the ends to 3–5mm (0.12–0.2 in).

14

A finished backside stitch, inside (left) and outside (right).

15

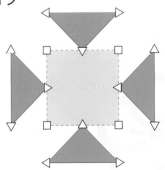

Now let's look at the next pattern, which is a little more complicated.

16

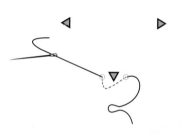

Start with the triangles, which need frontside stitches. Make a 2mm (0.08in) stitch underneath the point.

17

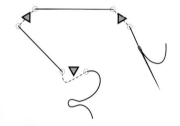

The thread runs over the fabric to the next point. Make 2mm (0.08in) stitches under each point.

18

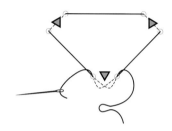

When you get to the end of the loop, stitch once more under the first point.

19

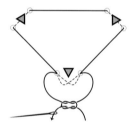

Tie 3–4 overhand knots, pulling each one tight. The corners will join up.

20

Trim the ends to 3–5mm (0.12–0.2in).

21

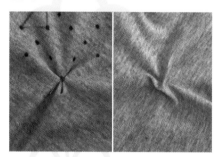

A finished frontside stitch, inside (left) and outside (right).

22

Locate the points from the inner square – after sewing the triangles the material will be distorted.

23

Sew a backside stitch (steps 9–13) using the points of the square.

24

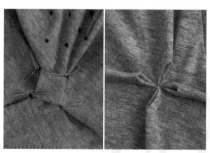

The finished blue pattern, inside (left) and outside (right).

25

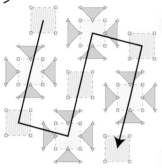

Complete the smocking, working from one pattern to the next as shown by the arrow.

26

The finished pattern inside. Trim all loose threads, checking you didn't miss any points.

27

The finished pattern from the outside. Try it on!

28

If you like, you can repeat the design on the other side of the t-shirt.

ADVANCED TIP

For a longer-lasting t-shirt, one that will survive more washes, stitch point to point. The arrows on the template show the points that should connect.

FOLD BITE 1

Folds can be dangerous – they will attack a garment and never let go! The following two pieces can be done with a sewing machine. The technique used is neither smocking nor pleating, but something in between.

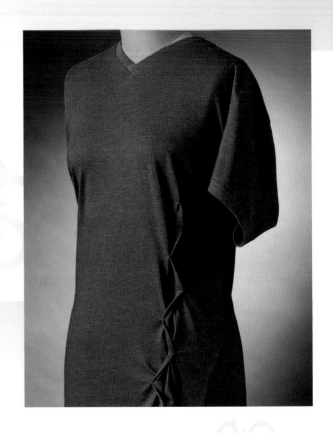

SHEET SIZE: N/A

FINISHED SIZE: A BIT SMALLER THAN YOU STARTED

MODEL: MATTHEW GARDINER

DIAGRAM: MATTHEW GARDINER

1

The first time you do this, use an inexpensive t-shirt or some scrap fabric to learn the technique.

2

First make a vertical mountain fold, to get the top layer on its own. Tip: pinch at the top and bottom of the fold and lift the shirt up.

3

Iron the crease flat.

4

Make a line of pins through both layers on an angle to your taste.

5

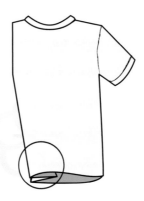

Turn the t-shirt inside out. Flatten the shirt out, paying attention to the fold inside.

6

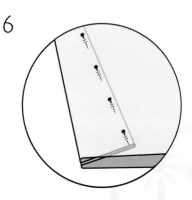

Take care to flatten out the angle on the inside. Pin into place.

7

The ' – x –' line shows where to sew. Sew as close as you can through all four layers of fabric.

8

Sew up to the top of the fold. Turn the t-shirt right side out.

9

5cm

Make small marks along the edge of the flap, 5cm (2in) apart.

10
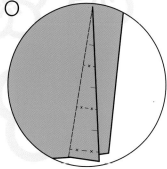

Sew along every second line.

11
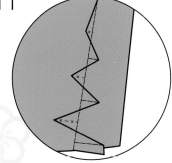

Stretch the fabric in the other direction on every second mark. Extra fold lines are formed, but not shown here for clarity.

12
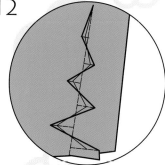

The extra folds coming from the stretching of the fabric are shown here.

13
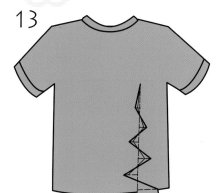

One fold-bitten t-shirt. You can also try this on other garments.

FOLD BITE II

Folds are even more dangerous in pairs – this garment has twice as much bite as the previous piece. These folds can be made in many kinds of garments, such as dresses, jackets or shirts. Be experimental.

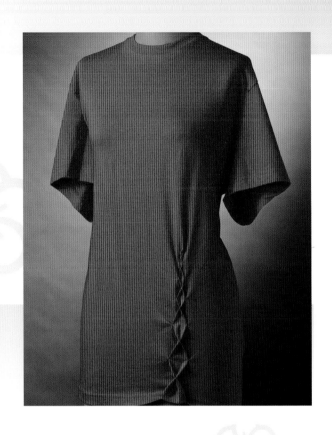

SHEET SIZE: N/A
FINISHED SIZE: A BIT SMALLER THAN YOU STARTED
MODEL: MATTHEW GARDINER
DIAGRAM: MATTHEW GARDINER

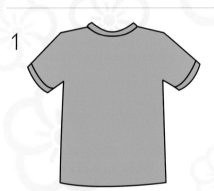

1

The first time you do this, use an inexpensive t-shirt or some scrap fabric to learn the technique. Cotton or blends work well; a little bit of stretch in the fabric is ideal.

2

First make a vertical mountain fold, to get the top layer on its own.
Tip: pinch at the top and bottom of the fold and lift the shirt up.

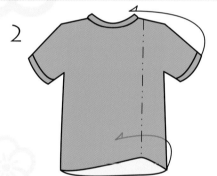

3

Make a 10–20° angle fold on the edge.

4

Iron the crease flat, then unfold.

5

Sew along the crease.

6

Flatten out the t-shirt to its normal shape, then make a squash fold on the flap.

7

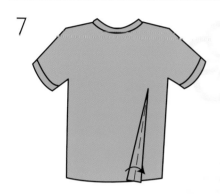

The flap is now squashed evenly on both sides of the sewn line. Fold it in half.

8

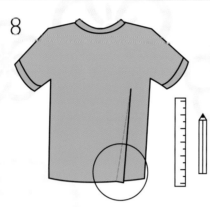

Get a pen or marker and a ruler. Make careful marks as follows.

9

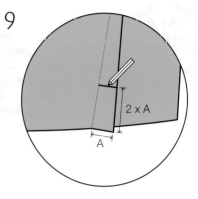

Measure the width of A. Then mark across the flap at 2 x A. e.g. if A = 3cm (1.18in), then 2 x A = 6cm (2.36in).

10

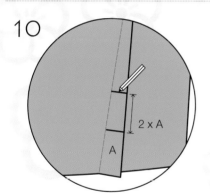

Repeat the measurement, but this time make A the width of the last mark. It will be a bit smaller.

11

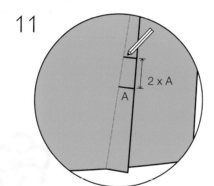

Repeat this process until you reach the point where the flap is 1cm (0.4in) wide. After this the folds will be too small to make.

12

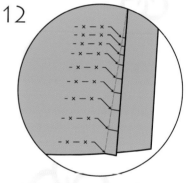

All the marks are made. Sew through the flap at each of these marks. Sew the flap at the bottom as well.

13

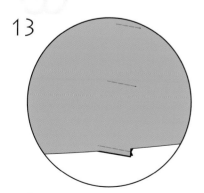

Sew the bottom flap to the t-shirt. Make small strong (holding) stitches on the edge at the midpoint between each sewn line.

14

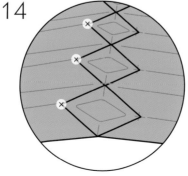

Stretch the midpoint of the top flap across and sew holding stitches on each feature.

15

Finish all holding stiches and the 'bite' will be formed by tension in the fabric.

CAFE PURSE

No outfit is complete without a handbag. This one can be folded from many materials, such as foil coffee bags, felt or synthetic leather. All it takes is a little bit of creativity.

SHEET SIZE: 30 X 30CM (12 X 12IN)
MATERIAL: COFFEE BEAN FOIL BAG (HDPE)
FINISHED SIZE: 11 X 15CM (4.3 X 5.9IN)
MODEL: MATTHEW GARDINER
DIAGRAM: MATTHEW GARDINER

1

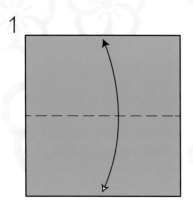

Book fold horizontally.

2

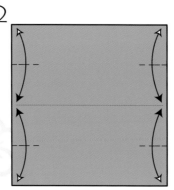

Make small creases at 1/4 marks.

3

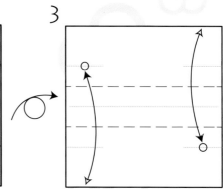

Make creases using edges and 1/4 marks as landmarks.

4

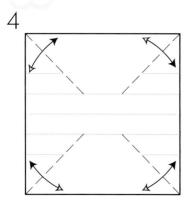

Fold all diagonals from the corners to the creases from step 3.

5

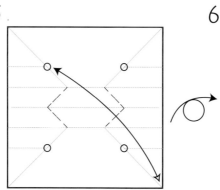

Make four small 45° creases, fold corners to marked points. Turn over.

6

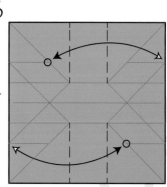

Make two vertical folds, being careful not to crease across the middle section.

FASHION
CAFE PURSE

7

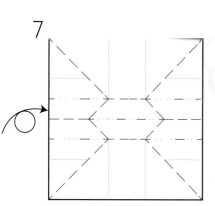

Collapse using folds shown.

8

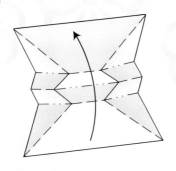

Collapse in progress. Fold the model in half to get to step 9.

9

The collapse is complete. The diagram shows the folds inside.

10

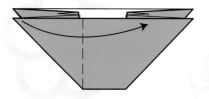

Fold the front flap across, using the bottom corner as a landmark.

11

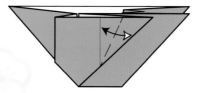

Pre-crease the point in preparation for a squash fold.

12

Squash fold the point.

13

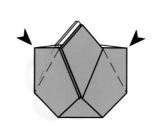

Repeat steps 10–12 on the three other flaps.

14

Pre-crease, then inside reverse fold the two corners.

15

Open the top of the purse a little then look in from above.

FASHION
CAFE PURSE

16

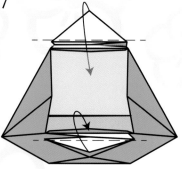

The view from above. Tuck the inner triangle flaps into the outer pockets.

17

Tuck the outer triangle flaps into the inner pockets. The model is now locked.

18

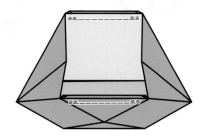

For a more robust purse, you can sew or glue along these seams.

19

Finished purse, ready to fill with riches.

DECORATIVE ORIGAMI

A cardboard form made with Gerald Priewasser's *flexible surface*, at the Ars Electronica Festival 2010.

DECORATIVE ORIGAMI

Origami can be used for a wonderful range of decorative projects, from wrapping books to interior design. This section takes you through a variety of projects, including a selection of fun boxes and covers and a stunning piece of wall art. These origami models use a range of materials, including paper, cardboard and even foil coffee bags!

amazing and will last longer if you use a more durable material, such as card, cardboard or plastic. Experiment with each model and material until you find the combination that you like best. When folding thicker materials, you will find it a lot easier to work with them if you first learn how to score them.

FROM PAPER TO PLASTIC

All of the models in this section can be created with paper, but many of them will look even more

START BY SCORING

Scoring means to make an incision or impression in the material that you want to fold without cutting

DECORATION
DECORATIVE ORIGAMI

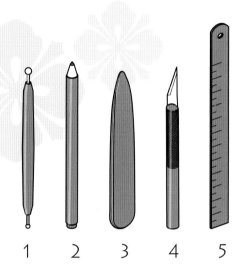

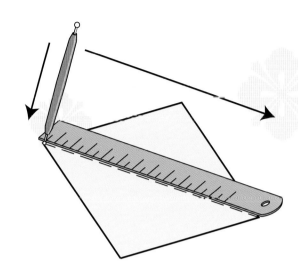

1   2   3   4   5

all the way through. Scoring before making a fold can reduce the chance of the material cracking, and has two advantages. Firstly, the fold will be 'programmed' into the material by the score. Secondly, the score will make the material thinner along the fold line, resulting in a sharper crease. The trick is to apply just enough force to make an impression in the material without damaging it.

SCORING TOOLS

The tools illustrated above are available in art and craft stores.

1. Embossing tool: a pen-like tool with rounded metal ends. For thicker material, use the larger end, for paper use the smaller end.
2. A ballpoint pen with no ink. The ballpoint can be used as an embossing tool.
3. Bone folder. A specially shaped tool made from bone or plastic.
4. A pen knife, for cutting material to size.
5. A metal ruler, to guide your scoring tool.

HOW TO SCORE PAPER AND CARD

Scoring is a simple matter of 'drawing' a line using a scoring tool. Use a ruler to guide the tool.

1. Place your scoring tool precisely at the start of the fold line.
2. Position the ruler beside the scoring tool and align the ruler along the fold line.
3. Press the scoring tool down.
4. Draw the scoring tool along the ruler to the end of the fold line. Keep the pressure constant.
5. Try folding along the line. Does the material fold easily? If not, more pressure is needed when scoring.
6. Was the paper torn or damaged? If so, use less pressure.
7. Practise steps 1–6 until you get a good result.

HOW TO SCORE CARDBOARD

The difference between card and cardboard is that cardboard is made of several layers. The basic type we find in packaging is made of two flat outer layers and an inner corrugated layer. If you try to fold cardboard without pre-scoring then you will end up with a fold that is not straight. The method is the same as scoring paper or card, but you need a tool with a larger head. Use a scoring tool with a radius that is at least twice the thickness of the cardboard. You may need to improvise with the handle of a kitchen knife, or to create a special tool from a bicycle wheel. The key is not to break the surface layer. It takes practice to get consistent results.

TOOLS TO SCORE CARDBOARD

1. A scoring tool: an embossing tool with a head at least twice the thickness of the cardboard. Thinner will work but the fold will be more challenging to make.
2. A metal ruler.
3. A pencil to mark the sheet if necessary.
4. A sheet of cardboard to practise with.

Follow steps 1–7 on the previous page to practise scoring cardboard.

HOW TO SCORE PLASTIC

When folding thin plastic, first make a small cut in the surface of the material on the mountain side of the fold and then bend along the cut line. See the Lighting section for a guide to working with thin plastic sheets.

A bicycle wheel transformed into a custom-made scoring tool

DECORATION
DECORATIVE ORIGAMI

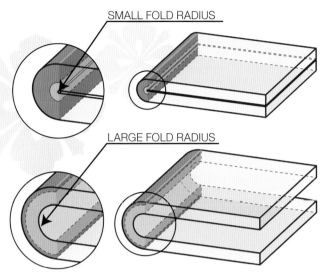

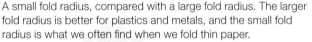

A small fold radius, compared with a large fold radius. The larger fold radius is better for plastics and metals, and the small fold radius is what we often find when we fold thin paper.

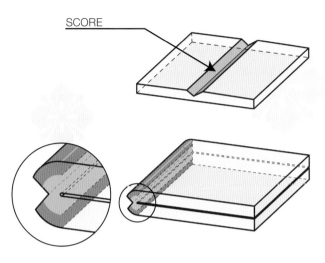

A score or cut in the sheet enables us to make sharper creases, with less stress, by reducing the thickness of the material along the fold line.

THE SCIENCE OF SCORING

When folding thicker materials, such as cardboard, plastic or even metal, it is important to consider the thickness of the material and the fold radius. The fold radius is the size of the inner circular shape we see along the fold line. Because paper is made from layers of fibres, it is easy to fold. The fibres separate when the paper is folded, allowing us to make sharp creases without cracking or tearing. Other materials, such as plastic and metal, have a tightly packed chemical structure that changes shape during folding. A fold creates two forces in the material during folding: compression and stretching.

The outer part of the fold stretches the material and the inner part of the fold compresses it. If the fold radius is too small, the material will stretch too much, causing it to crack. The image above shows two examples of fold radius size. Each fold

is marked with a dark colour on the outer edge to illustrate the amount of stretch, and a lighter colour along the inside of the fold to show the relative compression. The top fold shows a small radius, with a lot of stretch. If this fold was made in metal or plastic, the material would be close to cracking. The large radius shown in the bottom fold is ideal for metal or plastic. The radius is equal to the thickness of the material, so the outer edge is only slightly stretched.

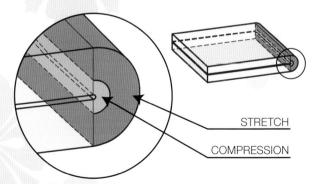

The darker shade on the outside shows where the material has stretched. The lighter colour in the centre of the fold shows where the material compresses.

CAFE WALLET

Recycle your foil coffee bags (HDPE) into a stylish and practical wallet. Designed to hold cards and cash, the wallet is both compact and functional. Stitching binds the wallet securely along key seams.

SHEET SIZE: A4: 21 X 29.7CM (8.26 X 11.69IN)
FINISHED SIZE: 10 X 7CM (3.93 X 2.75IN)
MODEL: MATTHEW GARDINER
DIAGRAM: MATTHEW GARDINER

1

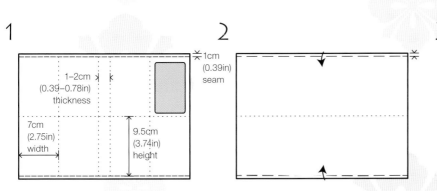

1–2cm (0.39–0.78in) thickness

1cm (0.39in) seam

7cm (2.75in) width

9.5cm (3.74in) height

The key dimensions are shown here. The design can be modified to be thicker or thinner, taller or wider.

2

Fold at 1cm (0.39in) to make seams along the top and bottom.

3

0.5cm (0.2in)

Sew both seams, then fold the bottom edge up to sit 0.5cm (0.2in) below the top edge.

4

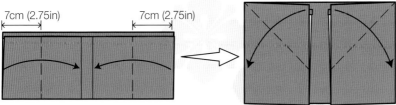

7cm (2.75in)   7cm (2.75in)

Fold each edge in 7cm (2.75in) towards the middle.

5

Fold each of the inner corners down on a 45° angle, taking the corners to the outer edges.

6

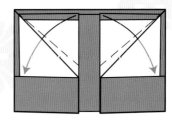

Fold the inner flaps in a similar way, adjusting the angle as shown.

7

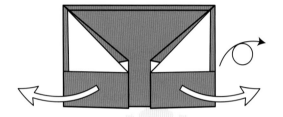

Open up the two flaps and turn over.

8

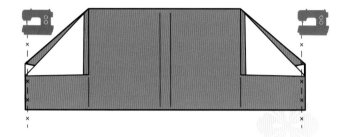

Sew through all layers on both outer edges.

9

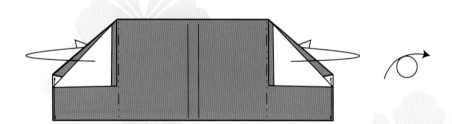

Mountain fold both flaps back into place, turn over.

10

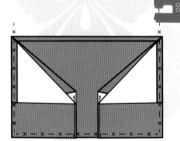

Sew along the three edges as shown.

11

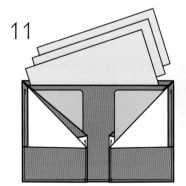

Money goes into the back pocket. Cards go into the front pockets.

12

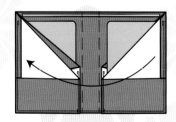

Make two valley folds to shape the thickness of the wallet.

13

Completed wallet.

JAPANESE BOOK WRAPPING

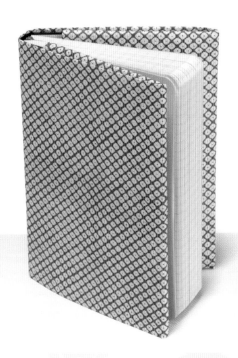

Wrapping books is a commonplace way to protect a book and disguise what you are reading. It uses a quick technique that requires no glue. Give special books some extra care with a decorative paper wrapping.

SHEET SIZE: 3 X BOOK WIDTH, 2 X BOOK HEIGHT
FINISHED SIZE: SAME SIZE AS THE BOOK
MODEL: TRADITIONAL, JAPAN
DIAGRAM: MATTHEW GARDINER

1

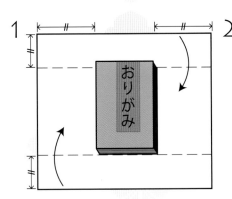

Place the book in the centre of the sheet. Mark and then fold the paper along the top and bottom edges of the book.

2

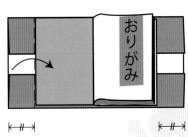

Open the front cover of the book then centre the book on the sheet. Fold the outer edge over the front cover.

3

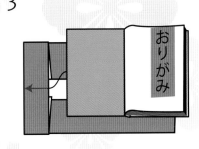

Lift the book up and slide the front cover inside the pocket.

4

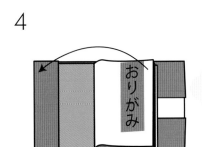

Like this. Open to the last page of the book.

5

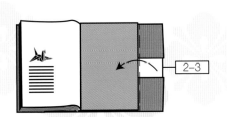

Repeat steps 2–3 on the back cover.

6

All done! A simple, fast and glue-free covering. Use patterned paper for a decorative effect.

QUICK CD COVER

Functional and decorative, this quick CD cover takes less than a minute to fold and will protect your CD from dust and scratches. Just add a cardboard insert and you can also use your cover as an envelope and send it in the post.

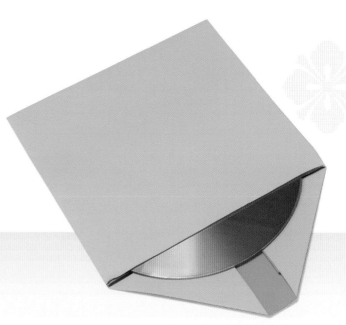

SHEET SIZE: A4: 21 x 29.7CM (8.26 X 11.69IN)
FINISHED SIZE: 12 X 12CM (4.72 X 4.72IN)
MODEL: MATTHEW GARDINER
DIAGRAM: MATTHEW GARDINER

1

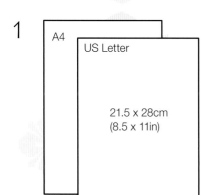

An A4 or US Letter (8.5 x 11in) sheet will work for this CD cover.

2

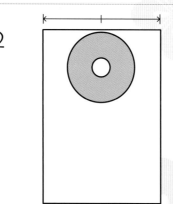

Place a CD in the centre of the paper, at the top.

3

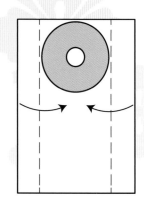

Fold the long edges inwards over the CD.

4

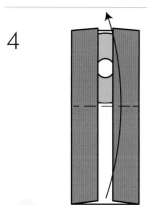

Fold the bottom edge upwards, along the bottom of the CD.

5

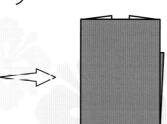

Like so. Turn over.

6

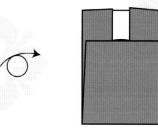

From this step we can choose to make one of two products: postable or re-usable.

POSTABLE

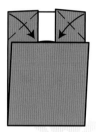

Fold top corners down to line up with the top of the CD.

7A

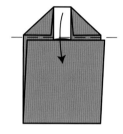

Fold the top edge down.

8A

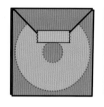

Origami House
Bunkyo-ku Tokyo
1-33-8-216
113-0001 JAPAN

The completed postable cover. Seal with tape or a sticker before posting.

RE-USABLE

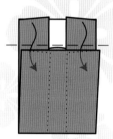

Fold the top edge down and tuck into two flaps to lock.

7B

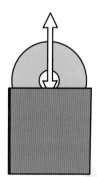

Finished CD cover. Decorate and re-use.

A4 ENVELOPE

This design transforms an A4 sheet into a postable envelope, making it possible to write a short letter on a single sheet and then fold the sheet into an envelope, ready for posting.

SHEET SIZE: A4: 21 × 29.7CM (8.26 × 11.69IN)
FINISHED SIZE: 8.5 × 12CM (3.34 × 4.72IN)
MODEL: OLGA SOUKHAREVSKY
DIAGRAM: OLGA SOUKHAREVSKY

1

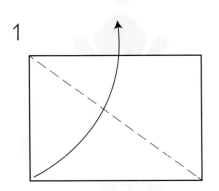

Fold your sheet along the diagonal.

2

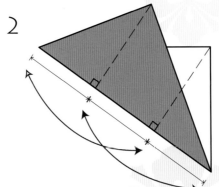

Crease at right angles to the bottom edge, in line with the top corners.

3

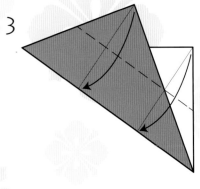

Valley fold corners to meet the bottom edge.

4

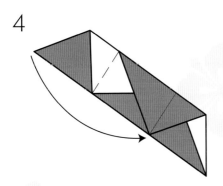

Fold on existing crease.

5

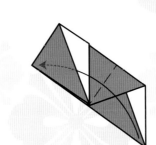

Fold on existing crease and tuck the point into the pocket created by the fold made at step 4.

6

The completed envelope.

POSTCARD BIRD

This decorative card features a geometrically charming bird. The card can be used for special occasions or invitations. Use a two-toned sheet of paper or card for the nicest results.

SHEET SIZE: A4: 21 X 29.7CM (8.26 X 11.69IN)
FINISHED SIZE: 10.5 X 19.2CM (4.13 X 7.55IN)
MODEL: OLGA SOUKHAREVSKY
DIAGRAM: OLGA SOUKHAREVSKY

1

Fold the sheet in half horizontally. Rectangular formats other than A4 will also work

2

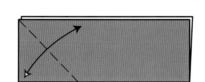

Valley fold and unfold on the diagonal, as shown.

3

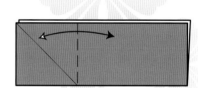

Make a vertical crease at the end of the diagonal crease.

4

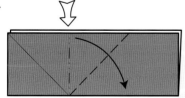

Squash fold.

5

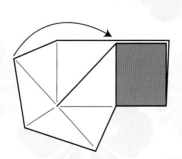

The squash fold in progress.

6

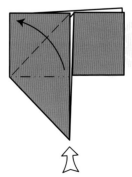

Squash fold again.

7

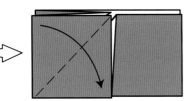

Valley fold and unfold on existing crease.

8

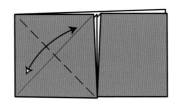

Valley fold and unfold across the diagonal.

9

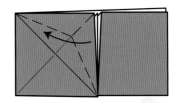

Rabbit ear fold.

10

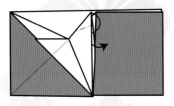

Inside reverse fold the point to form the bird's beak.

11

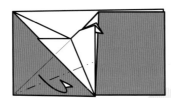

Mountain fold the top layer behind.

12

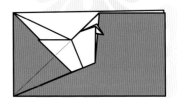

The finished postcard bird.

BIRD OF PARADISE

A classic napkin fold, with the addition of a stem, transforms colourful sheets of paper into decorative blossoms. Make a bunch of these birds of paradise for a table decoration.

SHEET SIZE: BLOSSOM: 15 X 15CM (6 X 6IN)
SHEET SIZE: STEM: 15 X 30CM (6 X 12IN)
FINISHED SIZE: 10 X 21CM (3.93 X 8.26IN)
MODEL: TRADITIONAL, MATTHEW GARDINER
DIAGRAM: MATTHEW GARDINER

1
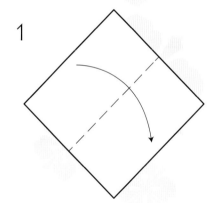
Begin with the paper white side up. Book fold in half, top to bottom.

2
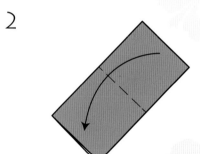
Book fold in half again, top to bottom.

3
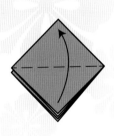
Fold upwards across the diagonal.

4
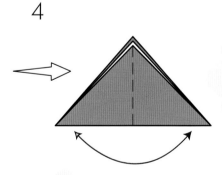
Crease along the centre line.

5
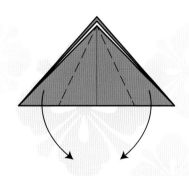
Fold outer points to meet along the centre line.

6
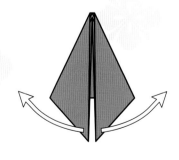
Open up the last folds a little.

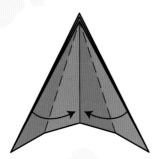

7

Valley fold the top layer only, bringing the edges to the centre line.

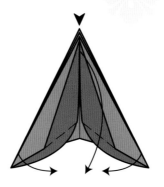

8

It will form a point. Lift the point upwards, making a reverse fold.

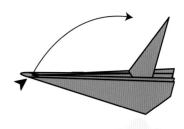

9

Rotated side view. Repeat steps 7–8 with the next layer to form the next petal.

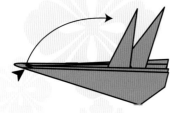

10

Repeat steps 7–8 with the next layer to form the next petal.

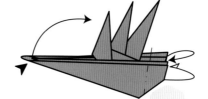

11

Repeat steps 7–8 with the next layer to form the next petal. Fold edges on both sides inwards as shown.

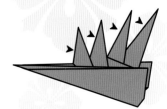

12

Once all the petals are folded, add some natural curves to each petal (see the model photo for ideas).

STEM

Use a 2:1 sheet for the stem. The shortest side should be the same length as the sheet used to make the flower. Fold in half lengthways.

14

Fold and unfold the top layer corner to corner.

15

Valley fold the top layer.

16

Valley fold to meet the crease made in step 14.

17

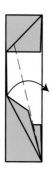

Valley fold on the crease from step 14.

18

14–17

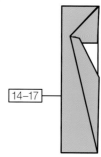

Repeat steps 14–17 on the other side.

19

Inside reverse fold in line with the folded edge on the top layer.

20

Inside reverse fold in line with the angle of the folded edge.

21

The stem is complete.

22

Place a flower into the open valley at the top of the stem, positioning the flower as shown.

23

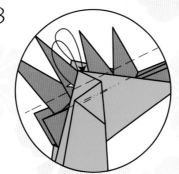

Fold the upper point of the stem into the pocket of the flower, locking the flower in place.

24

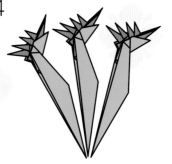

Fold more blossoms and stems to make a bunch.

FOUR-LEAF CLOVER BOWL

Count your lucky folds! This delightful bowl is perfect as a vessel for little knick-knacks around the house. Try folding the bowl from a larger sheet of heavier paper stock to make your luck last longer.

SHEET SIZE: 15 X 15CM (5.9 X 5.9IN)
FINISHED SIZE: 6.5 X 6.5CM (2.55 X 2.55IN)
MODEL: EVI BINZINGER
DIAGRAM: EVI BINZINGER

1

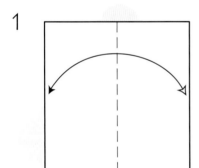

Book fold in half and unfold.

2

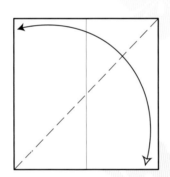

Crease across the diagonal.

3

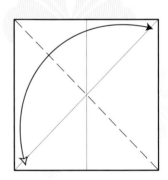

Crease across the other diagonal.

4

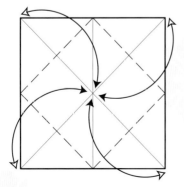

Blintz fold all corners to the centre and unfold.

5

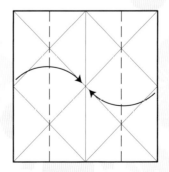

Valley fold the side edges to the centre crease.

6

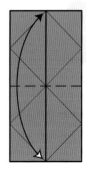

Book fold in half vertically and unfold.

7

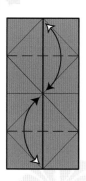

Valley fold the top edges to the centre crease and unfold.

8

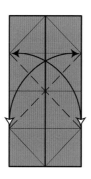

Crease diagonally through the centre.

9

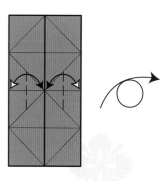

Make creases as shown, folding both sides to the centre.

10

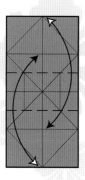

Valley fold and unfold as shown.

11

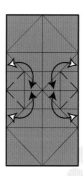

Valley fold and unfold through all layers, creasing as indicated.

12

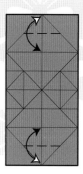

Valley fold and unfold through all layers, creasing as indicated.

13

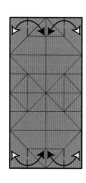

Valley fold and unfold through all layers, creasing as indicated.

14

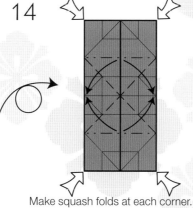

Make squash folds at each corner.

15

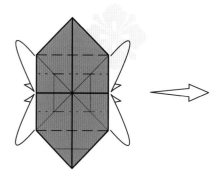

Pleat, forming mountains and valleys as shown.

16

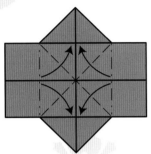

Lift the inner edges outwards,
forming a box shape.

17

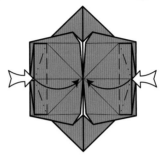

3D view. Squash fold the inner layer
to the centre of the model.

18

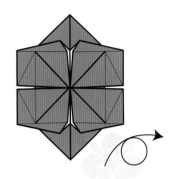

Like so. Turn over.

19

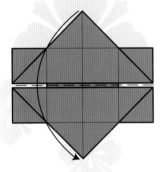

Valley fold top to bottom.

20

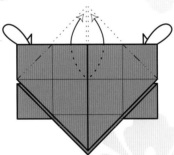

Pull up a layer of paper from behind
and mountain fold the corners.

21

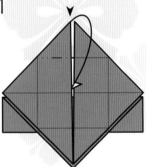

Reverse fold the point inside the
model.

22

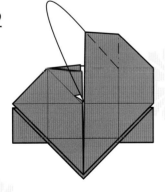

Repeat on the other side.

23

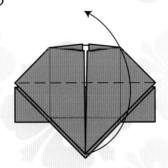

Valley fold upwards.

24

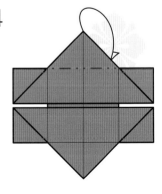

Mountain fold behind and insert into
the pocket.

25

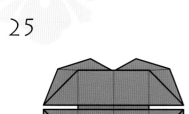
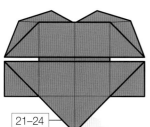

21–24

Repeat steps 21–24 on the bottom side.

26

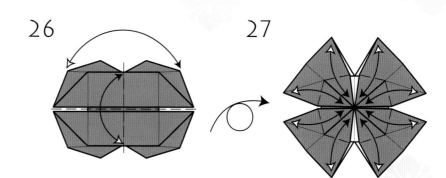

Fold and unfold horizontally and vertically. Push the centre point upwards to balance the petals' shape.

27

Fold all points to the centre and unfold.

28

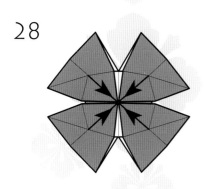

Curve all points towards the middle to round the bottom of the bowl.

29

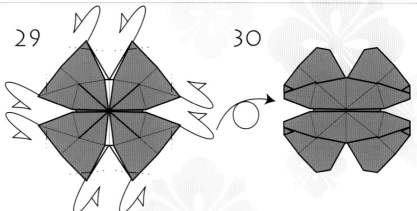

Fold the points behind to shape the leaves.

30

Sink fold the points to hide them. The result will look like this.

31

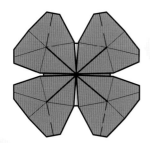

If you like, add extra creases to make the model look symmetrical.

32

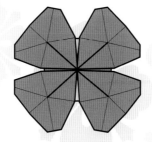

The finished four-leaf clover bowl.

BOX FOR GINA

This box has a delicate closing mechanism that is that is best left shut once folded. The box is perfect for potpourri or other fragrant herbs to spice up your home. Try folding a large box with thin card.

SHEET SIZE: 15 X 15CM (5.9 X 5.9IN)
FINISHED SIZE: 7.5 X 7.5CM (2.95 X 2.95IN)
MODEL: EVI BINZINGER
DIAGRAM: EVI BINZINGER

1

Begin white-side up. Book fold in half horizontally and vertically.

2

Fold all corners to the centre and unfold.

3

Crease by folding the edges to the centre on all sides.

4

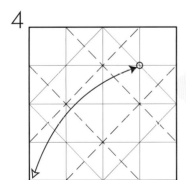

Crease by folding each corner to the 1/4 mark intersection on the opposite side.

5

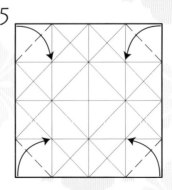

Valley fold all corners inwards.

6

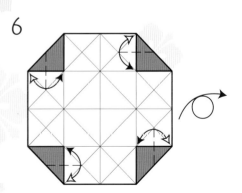

Crease at each corner as shown. Turn over.

7

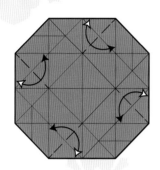

Crease on each side as shown.

8

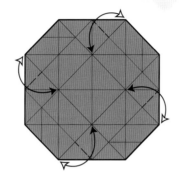

Crease on each side as shown.

9

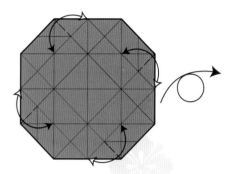

Crease on each side as shown.

10

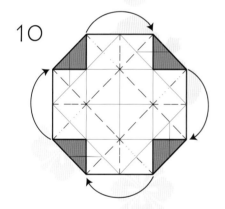

Form a 3D box, using the creases indicated.

11

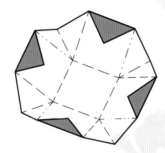

Step 10 in progress.

12

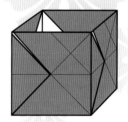

The box shape is formed.

13

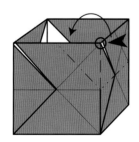

Push the corner inwards and down along creases shown.

14

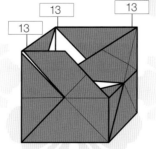

Repeat step 13 on the remaining three corners. The lock is very fragile, this step takes patience.

15

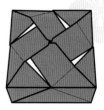

The completed box.

CARSON'S BOX

This box has a twist and a decorative windmill-style top. Use a decorative sheet of paper to create a beautiful box that is perfect for jewellery or other small treasures.

SHEET SIZE: 15 X 15CM (5.9 X 5.9IN)
FINISHED SIZE: 6.5 X 6.5CM (2.55 X 2.55IN)
MODEL: EVI BINZINGER
DIAGRAM: EVI BINZINGER

1
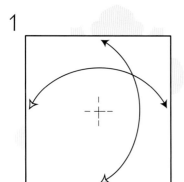
Book fold horizontally and vertically, pinching a small crease in the centre.

2
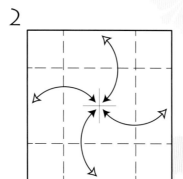
Fold each edge to the centre and unfold.

3
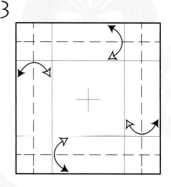
Make 1/8th creases as shown.

4
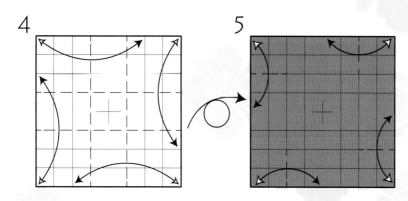
Make creases as shown. Turn over.

5
Valley fold to reverse the crease direction.

6
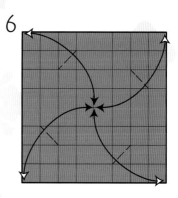
Make small creases as shown.

7

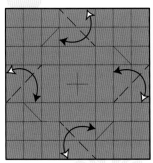

Make four small creases as shown.

8

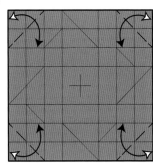

Make four small creases as shown.

9

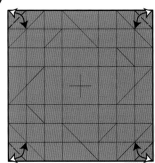

Make four small creases as shown.

10

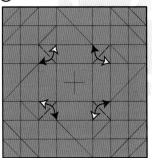

Make four small creases as shown.

11

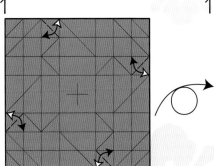

Make four small creases as shown.

12

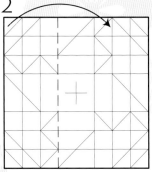

Valley fold on the third crease from the left.

13

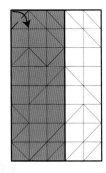

Fold in the small corner.

14

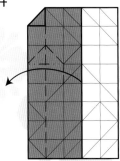

Fold back to the left, forming a 3D shape using creases shown.

15

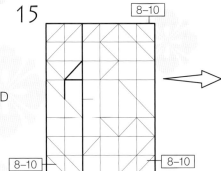

Repeat steps 8–10 on the remaining three sides.

16

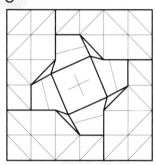

The resulting 3D object looks like this.

17

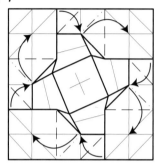

Focusing on one edge at a time, twist the corners into place.

18

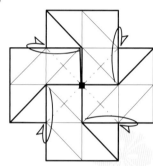

Mountain fold on the layer below and tuck the point in under the fold.

19

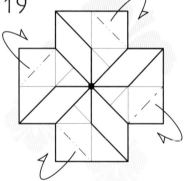

Fold the point behind on each corner.

20

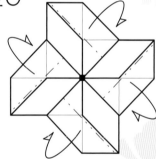

Fold each flap behind. Each one will fit neatly into a pocket underneath.

21

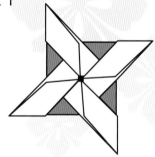

The finished box viewed from the top.

22

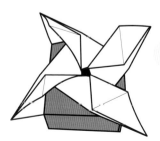

A side view of the finished box.

CHOPSTICK HOLDER

I nspired by a traditional chopstick holder, this holder has a small lock to keep the chopsticks in place. This chopstick holder is the perfect addition to your next dinner party.

SHEET SIZE: 15 × 15CM (5.9 × 5.9IN)
FINISHED SIZE: 16 × 5CM (6.29 × 1.96IN)
MODEL: MATTHEW GARDINER
DIAGRAM: MATTHEW GARDINER

1

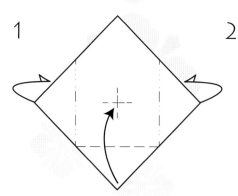

Make pinches to mark the centre. Valley fold the bottom point, then mountain fold the side points behind.

2

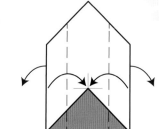

Fold the two sides to the centre. The points behind will swing to the front.

3

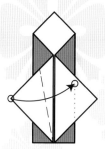

Fold one corner to meet the vertical edge underneath.

4

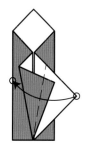

Repeat on the other side.

5

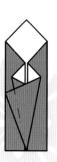

Mountain fold the overhanging edge behind the fold created at step 3.

6

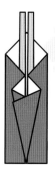

The chopstick holder is complete. Use decorative paper for a special occasion.

TATO COASTER

This coaster has a decorative folded pattern that can be enhanced with a patterned sheet of paper and protected with a coat of varnish or lacquer. It can also be used as a traditional Japanese purse.

SHEET SIZE: 20 X 20CM (7.87 X 7.87IN)
FINISHED SIZE: 10 X 10CM (3.9 X 3.93IN)
MODEL: TRADITIONAL, JAPAN
DIAGRAM: MATTHEW GARDINER

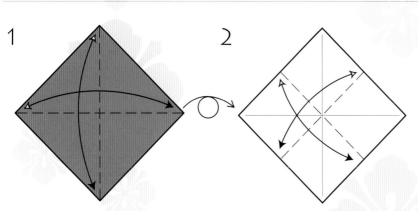

1

Start with the coloured side up.
Fold and unfold diagonals. Turn over.

2

Book fold and unfold.

3

Collapse into the preliminary base.

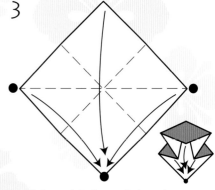

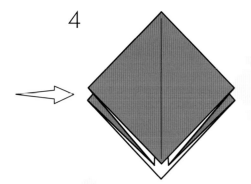

4

The preliminary base.

5

Fold the edges of the top layer to
the centre.

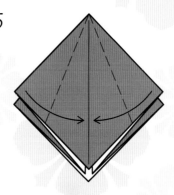

6

Repeat step 5 on the other side.

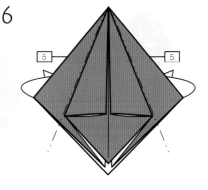

7

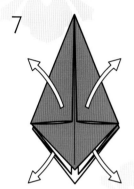

Unfold to a flat sheet.

8

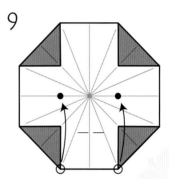

Fold the corners in at the intersection of existing creases. This makes a perfect octagon.

9

Fold the bottom edge to the centre. Be careful to only crease as shown.

10

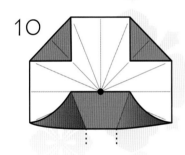

Step 9 in progress. Only crease between the dotted lines.

11

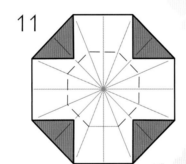

Repeat step 9 all around the octagon.

12

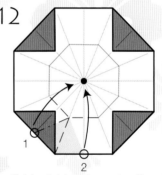

Fold point 1 to the centre, then fold point 2. This will create a point with the greyed out paper. Fold this point to the left. Look ahead to step 13 to see the result.

13

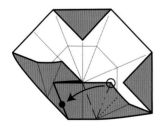

Fold the point marked by the circle to the point marked by the dot.

14

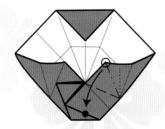

Repeat step 13 on the remaining points. The last point needs to be tucked under the first point.

15

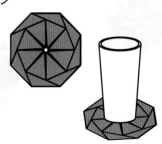

The finished tato. Protect with clear lacquer, then use as a coaster.

FLEXIBLE SURFACE

N ot many origami designs can be used in as many ways as this flexible surface. Decorate your home with this unique piece. Fold the model from a large sheet of cardboard and have fun experimenting with the possibilities.

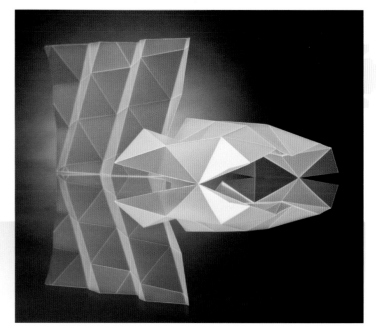

SHEET SIZE: 2:1 RECTANGLE OF CARDBOARD
FINISHED SIZE: VARIABLE
MODEL: GERALD PRIEWASSER
DIAGRAM: MATTHEW GARDINER

1

This guide helps you select the final number of triangles. For example, 5x3 is five triangles wide and three high. The variations: 3x2, 5x3 and 7x4 all fit neatly on a 2:1 sheet.

2

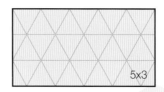

We will use 5x3 as an example. Measure the length and width of your 2:1 sheet, then calculate a division by 5 and a division by 3.

3

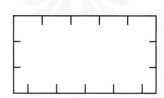

Mark even divisions on the sheet, as shown. On the bottom edge they will be offset by one half of a division.

4

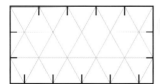

With a pencil carefully mark the fold lines between the marks, as shown.

5

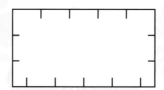

Follow the scoring method for cardboard outlined on page 3, and score all of the lines.

6

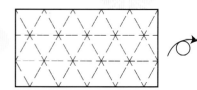

Valley fold on all score lines (arrows are not shown). Turn over.

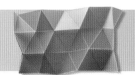

7

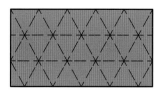

Valley fold on all fold lines again. This will make the sheet very flexible along the creases.

8

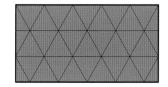

Now the model is complete, and you can begin experimenting with shapes you can make with this form.

9

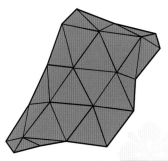

Try an organic form.

10

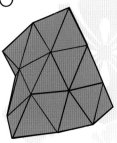

Try a geometric form.

11

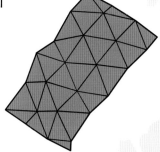

Try a minimal form.

ALTERNATIVE

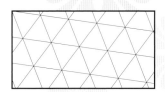

Folding the triangle pattern on a slight angle means the finished model can be made into a greater variety of shapes

CASCADE WATER WALL

Transform your spare cardboard boxes into stunning wall art for your home. With an extremely simple folding sequence and logical assembly, this model will allow you to cover a large wall surface stylishly and at minimal cost.

SHEET SIZE: 21 X 47CM (8.26 X 18.50IN)
FINISHED SIZE: 21 X 36.3CM (8.26 X 14.29IN)
MODEL: MATTHEW GARDINER
DIAGRAM: MATTHEW GARDINER

1

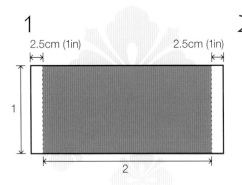

Begin with a 2:1 ratio sheet with an extra 2.5cm (1in) at each end.

2

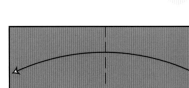

Book fold in half.

3

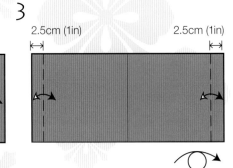

Mark 2.5cm (1in) with a ruler as shown, then make a firm crease at each end.

4

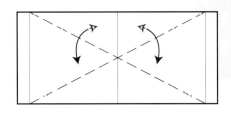

Make diagonal creases between the 2.5cm (1in) folds.

5

Form into a 3D shape by folding on existing creases.

6

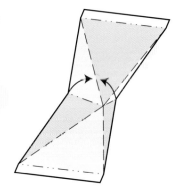

Bring the centre mountain folds together so that they touch.

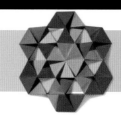

7

Valley fold the corners at the bottom, and mountain fold at the top.

8

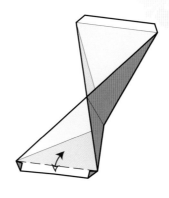

Valley fold on the crease at the bottom.

9

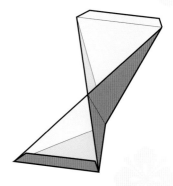

The finished unit.

10

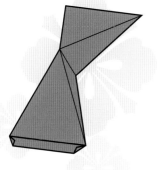

The finished unit viewed from above.

11

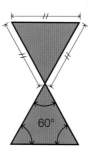

If we check the geometry of the triangles, all edges have the same length – we have equilateral triangles.

12

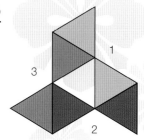

Because the edges are equal, we can form patterns of units on a flat surface, such as a wall. You will need three units.

THREE UNITS

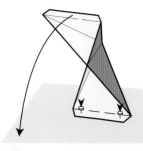

To mount, push two pins through the bottom flap into the wall. Fold towards the wall.

14

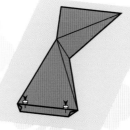

Adjust the shape so that the two centre folds are touching, then pin the opposite end into place.

15

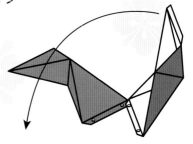

Place the next unit so that two corners are touching and the edges will align in its final position. Pin the flap, and fold down.

DECORATION

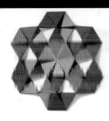

16

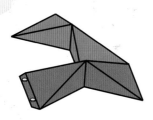

Pin the flap to the wall, making sure the two centre folds are touching.

17

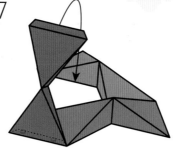

Place the next unit so that two corners are touching and the edges will align in its final position. Pin the flap, and fold down.

18

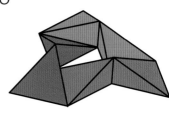

It will not be possible to pin the last flap, but you can insert it under the first unit and it will hold. Alternatively, use tape to secure it.

19

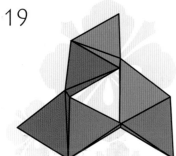

Three units assembled into a cascade.

MORE UNITS

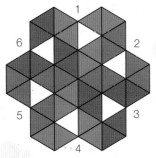

Several three-unit assemblies can be combined to make larger cascades. Six units combined will look like this.

ORIGAMI LIGHTING

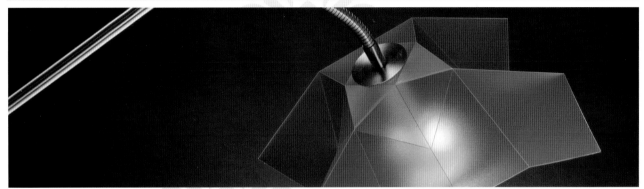

The liminal lamp on page 7 is made from folded polypropylene.

ORIGAMI LIGHTING

Origami can create an almost limitless number of extraordinary pieces of art. The creations are beautiful on their own, but imagine what happens when you take a folded shape and turn it into a light feature! These stunning origami lights will be the envy of all your friends – just wait until you announce that you made them yourself!

POLYPROPYLENE SHEET

The best material to use for origami lighting is polypropylene (PP). This is a versatile, strong, flexible plastic, which can be recycled. It is used as an engineering plastic, as well as for making items such as ropes, clothing, stationery and furniture. IKEA uses polypropylene to make some of their geometric lighting products.

A swatch of coloured polypropylene sheets.

The polypropylene you will need for origami lighting comes in sheets, which are available from most hobby, craft or art supply stores. The printing industry also uses polypropylene, so if you need a large quantity, try a printer who specialises in printing on plastics.

The sheet thickness is important: we use 0.3mm (0.01in) sheets, and usually buy them in A3-size sheets or larger. Polypropylene is available in a wide variety of colours, some translucent and some opaque. Both types work well for origami lighting, as even the opaque sheets let a lot of light through. Polypropylene is good for creating geometric shapes that do not have too many folds. If you try to fold more than three layers, the material becomes too thick, and the folds will not hold their shape. If this is the case, a little glue or mechanical fastening will keep them in shape.

SCORING POLYPROPYLENE

Polypropylene folds best if you use a craft knife and make a small cut in the surface first. This technique also works for most thin plastic sheets. Scoring polypropylene requires more pressure than scoring other plastics, as outlined in the scoring techniques in the Decoration section – in this case the knife actually cuts into the material. It is important to score the mountain side of the fold. The models in this chapter are not shown with this method specifically in mind, so if you are using this method, remember to score the mountain side of the fold.

YOU WILL NEED:

1. Pencil for marking the sheet
2. Craft knife for scoring
3. Metal ruler for guiding the knife

1

2

3

TECHNO ORIGAMI OPTION

If you have a CRAFT Robo cutter or other hobby cutter you can use it to score both simple and complex crease patterns in thin plastic.

MARKING BEFORE YOU FOLD

Use your pencil and ruler to mark the start and end of each fold before you make it. This will ensure your creases are accurate.

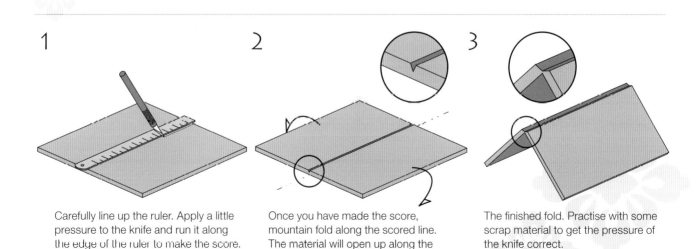

1 Carefully line up the ruler. Apply a little pressure to the knife and run it along the edge of the ruler to make the score.

2 Once you have made the score, mountain fold along the scored line. The material will open up along the fold line.

3 The finished fold. Practise with some scrap material to get the pressure of the knife correct.

TYPES OF LIGHTS

LED LIGHTS

LED (Light Emitting Diodes) are a popular form of lighting technology. They use minimal energy but emit a lot of light. The most practical LEDs are sold in a strip with adhesive backing, and are called LED flexible strips. This type of lighting is highly recommended for the lighting designs in this chapter. LED flexible strips are available from hardware, lighting and electrical stores.

LED flexible strips come in rolls. Each length is made up of smaller segments that can be cut at specific locations. The diagram to the right shows how three separate segments can be wired up. Connect the negative terminal at the end of one strip to the negative terminal on the next strip, doing the same for the positive terminals. The diagram also shows the soldered joints where the segments can be cut.

The strips are typically 4–5mm (0.16–0.2in) wide. The voltage is DC (direct current), so you will need a DC power supply to match the voltage and current recommended by the manufacturer. White lighting strips also come in a range of colour temperatures from cool (blue) white to warm (yellow) white.

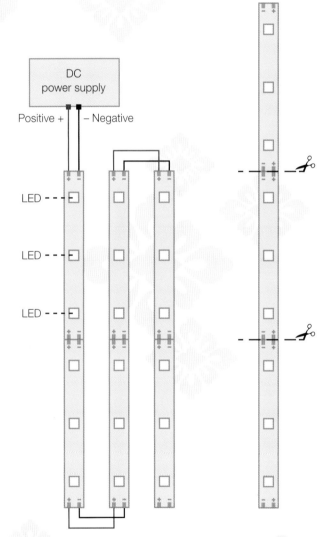

Left: An example of how three LED strip segments can be connected to allow for a lighting design that requires light in different locations. Positive (+) and negative (-) terminals are clearly marked on the strips. The red lines show the positive wires, the black lines show the negative wires.

Right: Locations where the strips can be cut. Joining the segments will require basic electronic knowledge and soldering skills, which is outside the scope of this book.

DC CONNECTORS

Many appliances use DC (direct current), and the power supplies usually have a similar kind of plug. If using LED lighting strips, it is best to use a plug that will directly connect to your DC power supply. There are a variety of shapes and sizes available at electrical hardware stores.

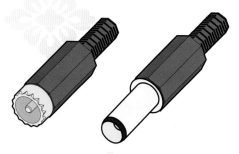

DC connectors make it easy to plug LED strip lighting into power. You will usually need to connect a female plug (left) to your strip of LEDs, using wire.

ECOBULBS

Ecobulbs are compact fluorescent lamps that have a long life and use less energy than incandescent bulbs. They are available in many different sizes and shapes, and fit into regular light fittings. These energy-saving light bulbs are recommended for lighting projects that need a lamp structure.

INCANDESCENT BULBS

Incandescent lights are commonly known as light bulbs. Incandescent bulbs are <u>not recommended</u> for these designs, as they can become very hot and could become a fire hazard when paired with paper or plastics. Although they are still available in some stores, they are being phased out of production in some countries due to their high energy use.

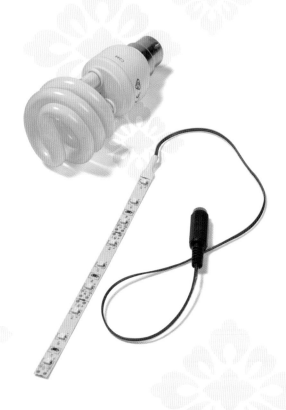

An standard Ecobulb and an LED strip with a DC power connector.

TWIST LAMP

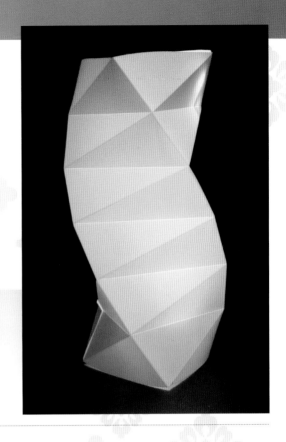

The twist lamp is made using a variation of a yoshimura pattern, and is designed to form a spiral. The lamp is best made in a thin-sheet plastic like polypropylene. It works well as a large cover over a table light, or as a replacement for a lampshade.

SHEET SIZE: 50 X 30CM (19.68 X 11.81IN)
FINISHED SIZE: 13.3 X 13.3 X 28.6CM (5.23 X 5.23 X 11.25IN)
MODEL: MATTHEW GARDINER
DIAGRAM: MATTHEW GARDINER

1

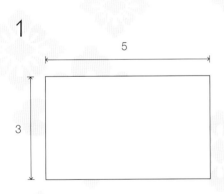

Use a large sheet with a 5:3 ratio.

2

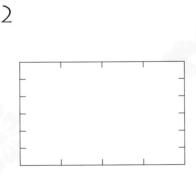

Make 1/4 marks on the top and bottom edge, and 1/6 marks on the sides.

3

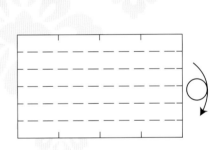

Score the horizontal lines.
Turn over.

4

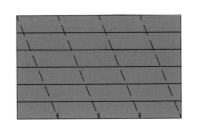

Score the diagonals between the 1/4 marks as shown.

5

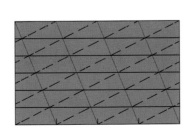

Score the diagonals across the intersections of existing scores, as shown.

6

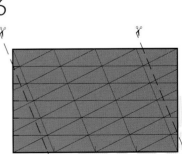

Trim the edges, leaving a 1cm (0.39in) gap outside the fold.

7

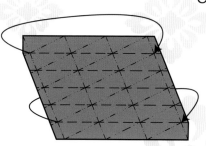

The completed pattern. Curve the sheet, forming a roll shape. The arrows show the intersections that will overlap.

8

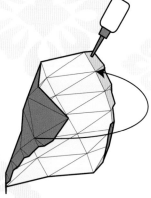

Apply glue to one edge. Bring the intersections together.

9

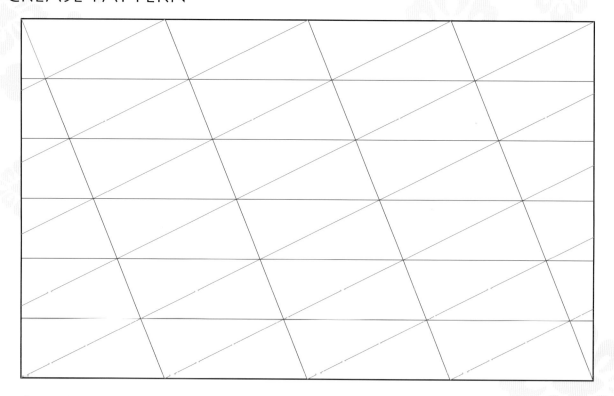

The finished twist lamp.

CREASE PATTERN

If you prefer, enlarge this pattern with a photocopier and use it as a guide to make your lamp.

LIMINAL LAMP

T he liminal lamp uses a few carefully placed folds to create a simple but elegant lighting shade. Fold a practice model using paper before moving on to the polypropylene model. Remember to score all folds first.

SHEET SIZE: 30 X 30CM (11.81 X 11.81IN)
FINISHED SIZE: 25 X 25 X 14CM (9.84 X 9.84 X 5.51IN)
MODEL: MATTHEW GARDINER
DIAGRAM: MATTHEW GARDINER

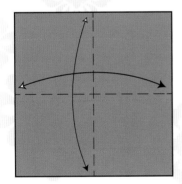

1

Mark and crease horizontally and vertically.

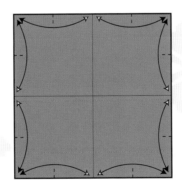

2

Pinch at the 1/4 marks on each edge.

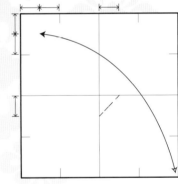

3

Fold a short diagonal crease to 1/8th from each corner. Refer to step 4 for the completed fold.

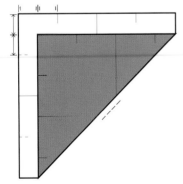

4

Step 3 in progress. Measure by eye and crease only at the centre of the fold, as indicated.

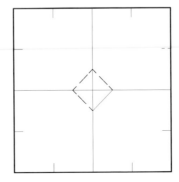

5

Repeat steps 3–4 on the other three sides.

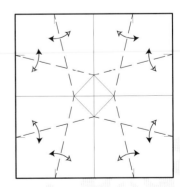

6

Fold between the corners of the middle square to the 1/4 marks on the outside edges.

7

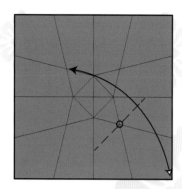

Make a crease at the intersection of the creases made in step 6. See step 8.

8

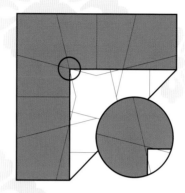

Be careful! The corner will be close to but not touching the intersection on the opposite side.

9

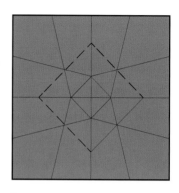

Repeat steps 7–8 on the remaining three sides.

10

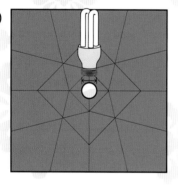

Cut a circle out of the centre to match the size of the light bulb base.

11

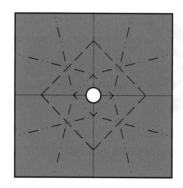

Fold on the creases as shown. The liminal light will become 3D.

12

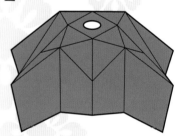

Shape the object to your liking by applying more pressure to selected folds.

13

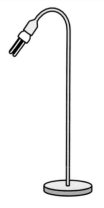

Find a simple lamp or light fitting like this one and remove the old cover.

14

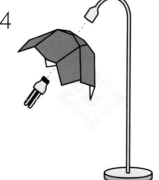

Assemble by inserting the bulb through the hole and into the socket of the lamp.

15

Enjoy your new liminal lamp.

CREASE PATTERN

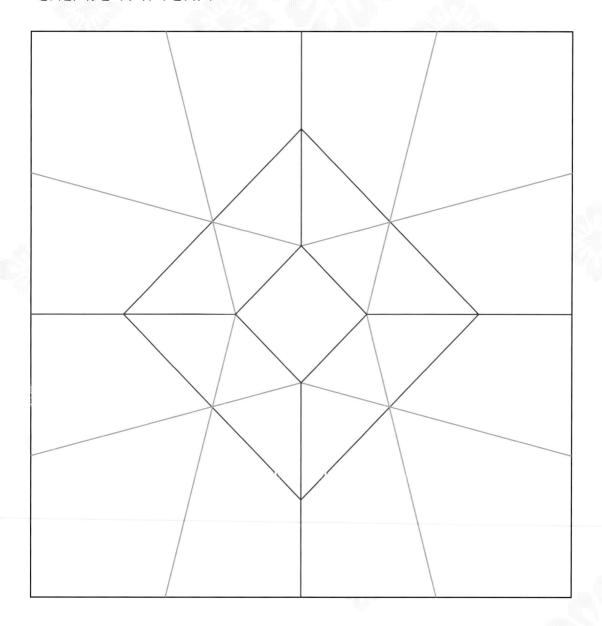

Copy this pattern at 200% to get a 30cm (11.81in) pattern. Overlay a sheet of transparent plastic such as polypropylene. Mark the fold lines and then score as shown on page 2 of this section. Then follow the instructional diagrams from step 10.

MASU PIXEL LIGHT

A masu is a traditional Japanese box. Here we repurpose the box to change it from a functional object into a decorative light fitting. You will need strip LEDs for light, and a simple frame to mount your pattern of masu pixels.

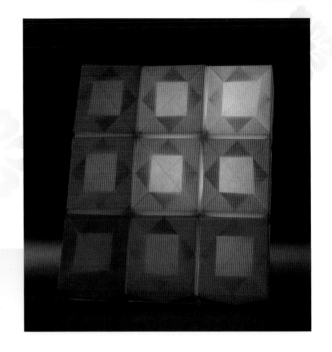

SHEET SIZE: 15 X 15CM (5.9 X 5.9IN)
FINISHED SIZE: 1 MASU: 5.3 X 5.3CM (2.08 X 2.08IN)
MODEL: TRADITIONAL, JAPAN, MATTHEW GARDINER
DIAGRAM: MATTHEW GARDINER

1
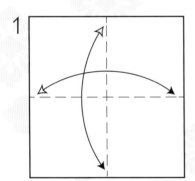
Fold and unfold diagonally.

2
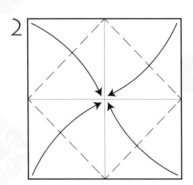
Fold all corners to the centre point. Rotate 45°.

3
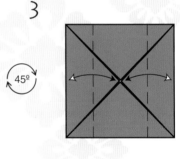
Fold the side edges to the centre.

4
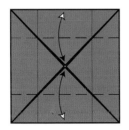
Fold the top and bottom edges to the centre.

5
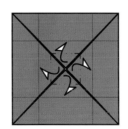
Mountain fold the points to the inner crease.

6
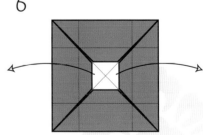
Unfold two side points.

7

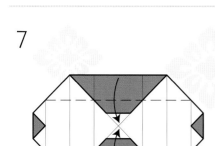

Fold on existing creases.

8

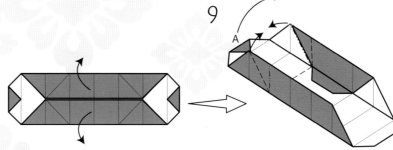

Lift sides to 90°.

9

To make the side of the box, lift point A upwards. The existing sides will naturally collapse to points.

10

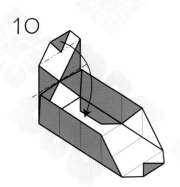

Fold the flap down into the box.

11

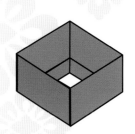

9–10

Repeat steps 9–10 on this flap.

12

Completed masu box.

13

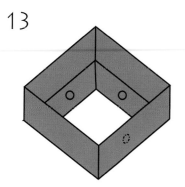

It needed, apply a little glue under the circled flaps.

14

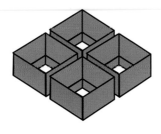

Make at least three more masu for a pixel grid.

LIGHTING
MASU PIXEL LIGHT

SIDE UNIT

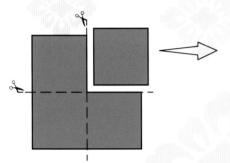

Cut a 1/4 sheet of paper for each side unit.

2

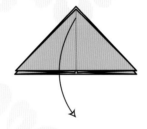

Follow steps 1–6 of the centre unit (see next page). Unfold the top layer.

3

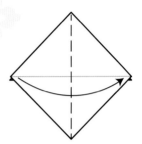

Fold the top layer across.

4

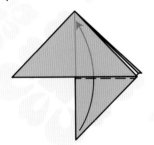

Fold the flap into the pocket.

5

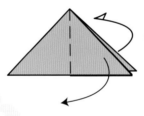

Rotate the flaps to 90° to make a three-pointed star.

6

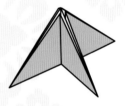

The finished side unit.

7

Use the side unit to join two boxes at one edge. Note: the masu pockets have two directions.

8

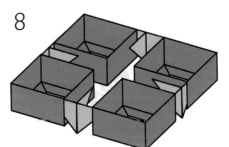

Fold three more side units and insert to construct a grid of four masu.

9

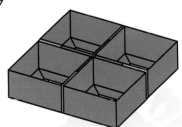

The completed grid.

CENTRE UNIT

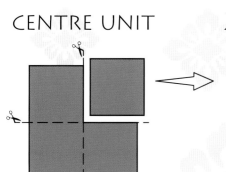

Cut a 1/4 sheet of paper for each centre unit.

2

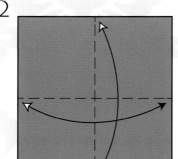

Book fold horizontally and vertically.

3

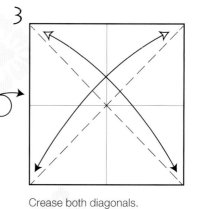

Crease both diagonals.

4

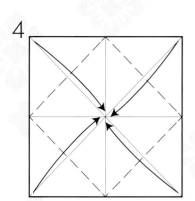

Blintz fold all corners to the centre.

5

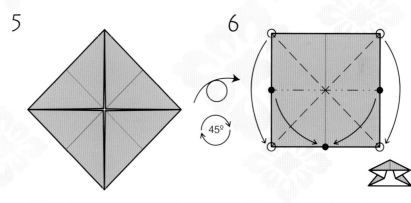

Like so. Rotate 45° and turn over.

6

Collapse into a waterbomb base.

7

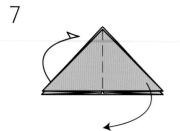

Rotate one flap at the back, and one flap at the front in the same direction.

8

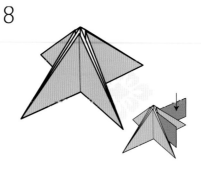

This is the centre unit; a four-pointed star with a pocket in each corner.

9

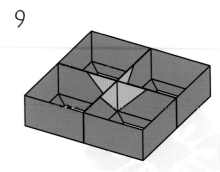

Place the centre unit in the middle of four masu.

BOTTOM UNIT

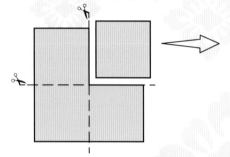

Cut a 1/4 sheet of paper for each bottom unit.

2

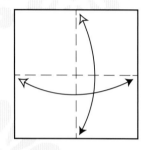

Book fold horizontally and vertically.

3

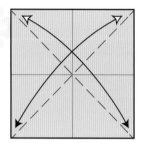

Crease both diagonals.

4

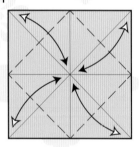

Blintz fold and unfold all corners to the centre.

5

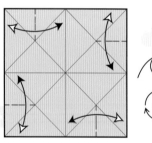

Fold the edges to the centre crease and only fold on the quarters shown.

6

Collapse into a preliminary base.

7

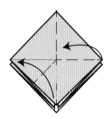

Swivel fold the bottom point to the side. The left side will rotate to 90°. The unit will become 3D.

8

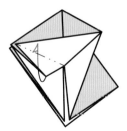

View from under the unit. Mountain fold fhe flap into the pocket.

9

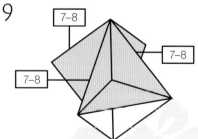

7–8

7–8

7–8

View from above. Repeat steps 7–8 on the other three sides. The last side is tricky.

10

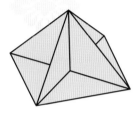

The finished bottom unit.

11

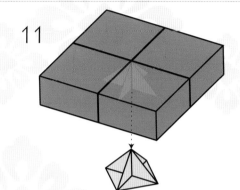

The bottom unit fits into the centre unit at the bottom of four masu boxes.

MOUNTING

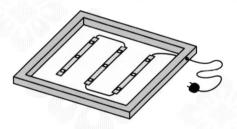

Buy or make a simple frame the same size as your grid of masu pixels. Mount some LED lighting strips with cabling.

2

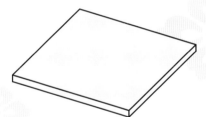

Prepare a sheet of white or opal acrylic sheet the same size as your masu pixels and frame.

3

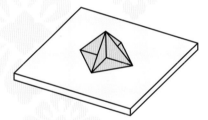

Glue the bottom unit in the centre of the acrylic sheet.

4

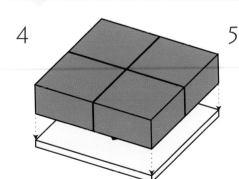

Place the masu pixels onto the bottom unit.

5

Switch on the power to check that everything works, then secure the origami and acrylic with glue or double-sided tape.

6

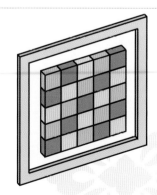

An alternative to LED lighting is to mount the masu pixels directly onto a window. Make as many as you like in your own composition.

SWEET LIGHT

This candy-shaped light uses an extremely simple crease pattern to create a geometric shape that looks fantastic when glowing from within. Use LED strips to light up the completed model. You will need press studs or velcro to finish it off.

SHEET SIZE: 5X4 RECTANGLE: 50 X 40CM (19.68 X 15.74IN)
FINISHED SIZE: 10 X 10 X 25CM (3.93 X 3.93 X 9.84IN)
MODEL: INSPIRED BY MASTER FUJIMOTO
DIAGRAM: MATTHEW GARDINER

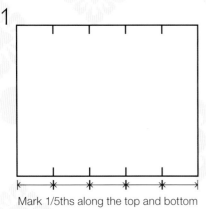

1. Mark 1/5ths along the top and bottom of the sheet.

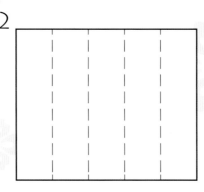

2. Make scores in the sheet at the 1/5th divisions.

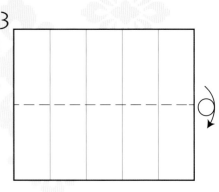

3. Mark and score horizontally across the centre. Turn over.

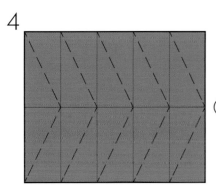

4. Carefully score the diagonals as shown. Turn over.

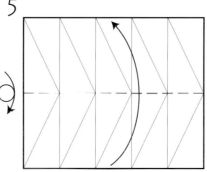

5. Fold in half.

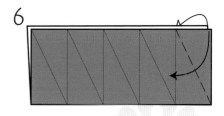

6. Valley fold in front and mountain fold behind.

7

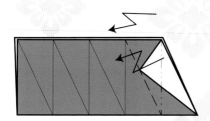

Outside crimp on the folds shown.
The folds on the back should mirror
the front.

8

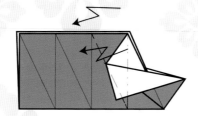

Outside crimp again.

9

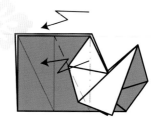

And again.

10

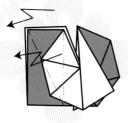

One last crimp, and the model will
overlap itself.

11

Now that all the folds have been made,
we can stretch the model into shape.

12

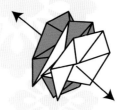

Hold both ends and gently stretch
the model.

13

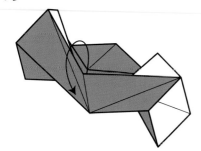

Keep stretching until it looks like this.
Lift the layer marked to the front.

14

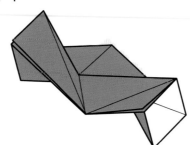

This is the finished form.

15

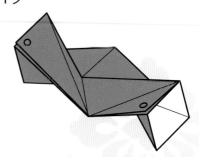

If you have press studs, make
holes and insert the studs at the
two circles.

16

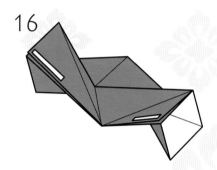

If you have velcro, stick it between the layers as shown. Unfold the model.

17

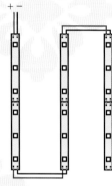

Prepare three short LED strips. Connect positive to positive and negative to negative between each strip.

18

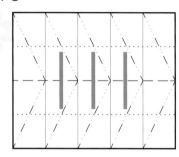

The purple lines show where to stick the LED strips inside the model.

19

Fold it back into its finished form and switch it on!

20

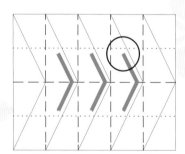

A slightly more complicated light strip arrangement.

21

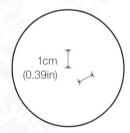

1cm
(0.39in)

Allow at least 1cm (0.39in) between the halfway line, the crease and the LED strip.

DARREN'S LANTERN

This light creates a lovely shadow and, if made with colourful sheets, can be used as a bright and warm lantern-style cover. This model uses origami paper, so take care to use a low-temperature light bulb, such as an LED or Ecobulb.

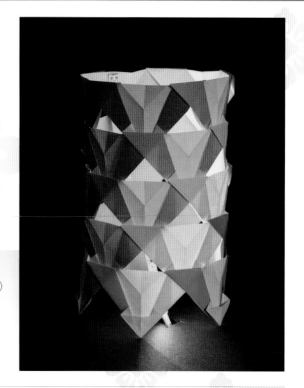

SHEET SIZE: 20 SHEETS: 15 × 15CM (5.9 × 5.9IN)
FINISHED SIZE: 17.5 × 16.5 × 23.8CM (6.88 × 6.49 × 9.37IN)
MODEL: DARREN SCOTT
DIAGRAM: MATTHEW GARDINER

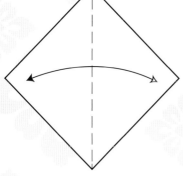

1

Begin white-side up. Fold and unfold along the diagonal.

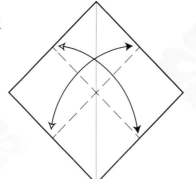

2

Fold and unfold sides.

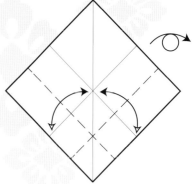

3

Fold and unfold to centre fold. Turn over.

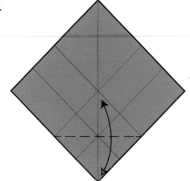

4

Fold bottom edge to centre. Turn over.

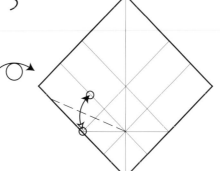

5

Fold and unfold.

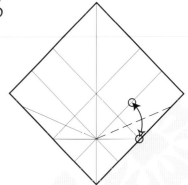

6

Fold and unfold.

7

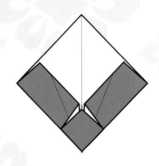

Insert left flap into the right flap.

8

Step 7 completed.

9

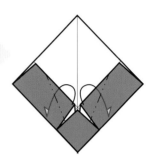

Mountain fold inside underneath the upper flap.

10

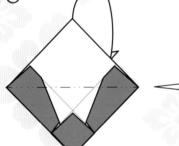

Mountain fold behind.

11

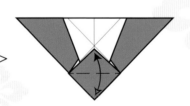

Fold and unfold.

12

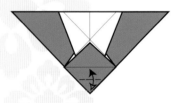

Fold and unfold.

13

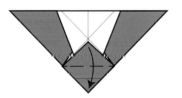

Fold down.

14

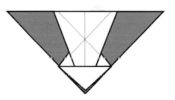

Unit completed. Make a total of 20 units, or more in multiples of five.

ASSEMBLY

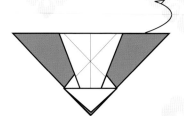

Unfold flap.

16

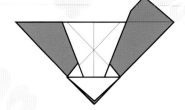

Like this.

17

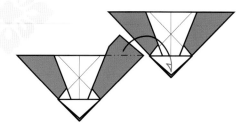

Insert flap inside another finished unit.

18

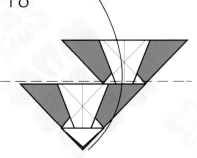

For the lock, lift the whole unit up.

19

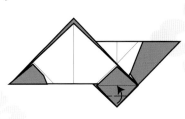

Fold all layers of the bottom edge upwards.

20

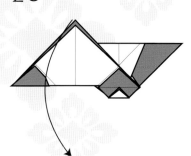

Fold the whole unit down again.

21

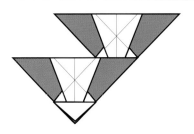

Two units assembled.

22

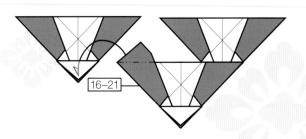

16–21

Add another unit.
Repeat steps 16–21.

23

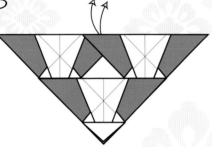

To lock the third unit with the one beside it, lift up the hidden flaps from both units.

24

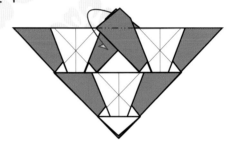

Insert the two flaps inside to lock on the top edge.

25

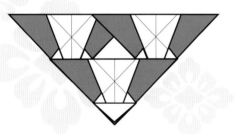

Three units completed.

26

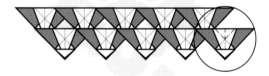

Assemble 10 units into a line. Shape the folds on each unit, as shown in the next step.

27

Crease the mountain and valley folds as shown. This will curve the line of units.

28

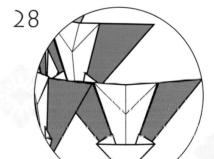

Like this.

29

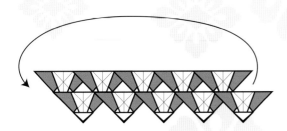

Curve the 10 units and join the units as shown in steps 16–21.

30

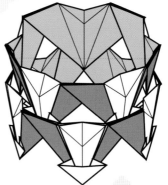

The result will look like this.

31

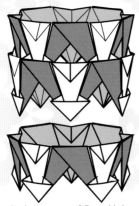

Make more units in groups of 5 and join each group to the bottom of the model, building up the basket shape.

32

Build up as many layers as you like. Place over a light or or mount onto an old wire light fitting.

KUSUDAMA LIGHT

Kusudama means 'medicine ball' in Japanese. When used as a light shade, the inner geometry of this model shows up beautifully. Use origami paper and a small LED or Ecobulb to light it.

SHEET SIZE: 6 SHEETS: 25 X 25CM (9.84 X 9.84IN)
FINISHED SIZE: 12.9 X 12.9 X 12.9CM (5.07 X 5.07 X 5.07IN)
MODEL: TRADITIONAL, JAPAN
DIAGRAM: MATTHEW GARDINER

1
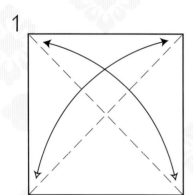

Begin white-side up.
Fold and unfold diagonals.

2
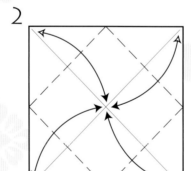

Blintz fold and unfold.

3
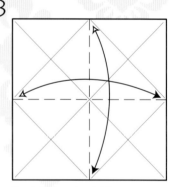

Book fold and unfold.

4
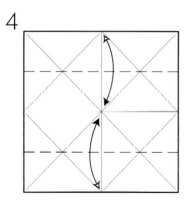

Cupboard fold and unfold.

5
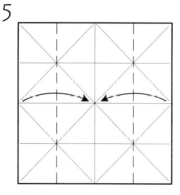

Cupboard fold.

6
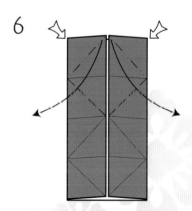

Squash fold using existing creases.

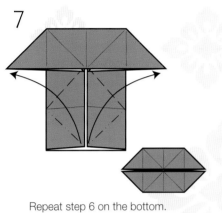

7

Repeat step 6 on the bottom.

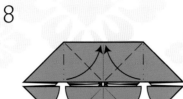

8

Squash fold.

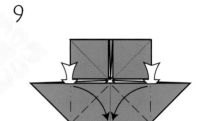

9

Repeat step 8 on the bottom.

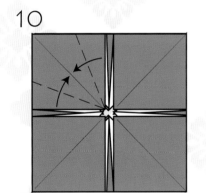

10

Valley fold.

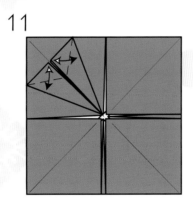

11

Fold and unfold.

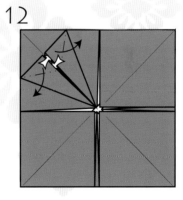

12

Squash fold on existing creases.

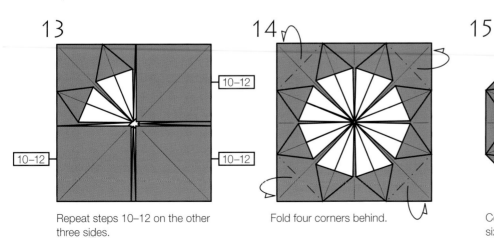

13

Repeat steps 10–12 on the other three sides.

14

Fold four corners behind.

15

Completed unit. Make a total of six units.

LIGHTING
KUSUDAMA LIGHT

16

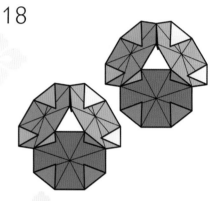

The following views are 3D. Turn over one unit.

17

Use glue to join the units together. Put the glue on the triangle tabs.

18

Glue together another set of three units to make two halves.

19

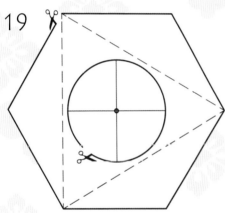

Photocopy or trace this shape onto thin-sheet plastic and cut out the shape and centre hole as marked. Valley fold on the dashed lines.

20

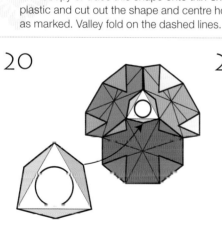

The centre hole is 27mm (1.06in), to fit a domestic-sized light bulb. Glue the plastic piece into the triangular hole.

21

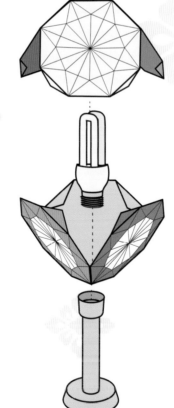

Assemble your light as shown. Glue the top section onto the bottom.

22

The finished kusudama light. You can fold a new model when you change the Ecobulb.

TACHI LAMP

T his lamp ingeniously flattens and expands. Not many lamps have such incredible mechanical properties! Try scoring the folds on thin-sheet plastic using the crease patterns before you start. Use LED or Ecobulb lights for best results.

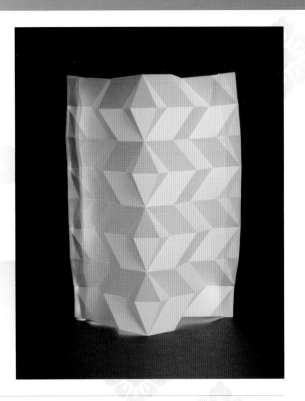

SHEET SIZE: 2 SHEETS: 30 x 30CM (11.81 x 11.81IN)
FINISHED SIZE: 27 x 27.8 x 10.9CM (10.6 x 10.9 x 4.29IN)
MODEL: TOMOHIRO TACHI
DIAGRAM: MATTHEW GARDINER

SIDE A

Crease in 1/4s horizontally.

2

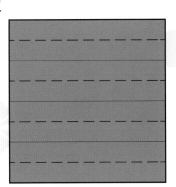

Crease along 1/8ths.

3

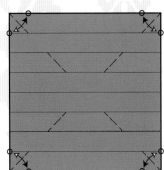

Crease between the 1/8ths shown by bisecting the corners.

4

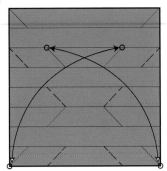

Crease between the 1/8ths shown by bringing the bottom corners to the 1/4 line.

5

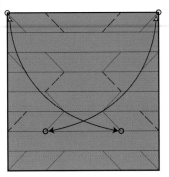

Repeat step 4 from the top edge.

6

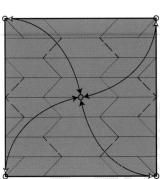

Crease between the 1/8ths shown by bringing the corners to the centre.

7

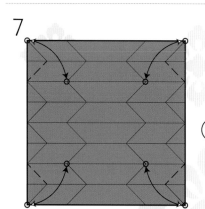

Crease between the 1/8ths shown by bringing the bottom corners to the nearest 1/4 line. Turn over.

8

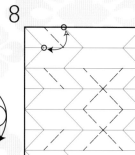

Crease between the 1/8ths shown by matching the crease end points.

9

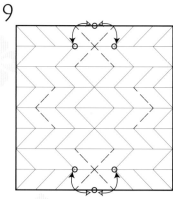

Crease as shown by matching the circle points to the edge.

10

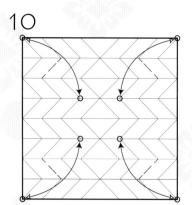

Crease between the 1/8ths by matching the corner to the 1/8th line as shown.

11

Bisect the folds at the edges.

12

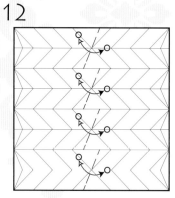

Match the diagonal crease onto the horizontal crease as shown.

13

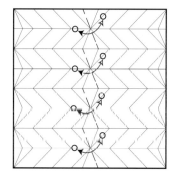

Match the diagonal crease onto the horizontal crease as shown.
Turn over.

14

Begin collapsing the crease pattern. Collapse one column of the zig-zag pattern at a time.

15

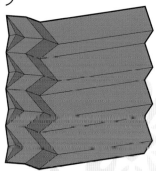

Four of the zig-zag patterns are shown here partially collapsed. Partially collapse the remaining pattern.

16

Once the pattern of folds is in place, completely collapse all folds.

17

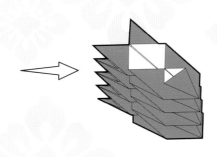

Side A is completed.

18

Take a new sheet and repeat steps 1–2. Fold the corners.

19

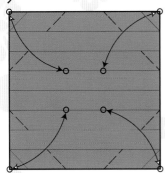

Crease between the 1/8ths by folding each corner to the 1/8th line as shown.

20

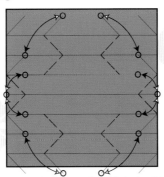

Crease between the 1/8ths by folding as shown.

21

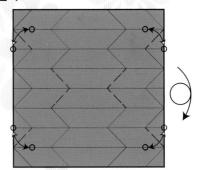

Crease between the 1/8ths by folding the 1/8th line to the edge. Turn over.

22

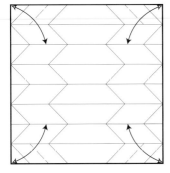

Crease between the 1/8ths by folding the corners to the neares 1/4 line.

23

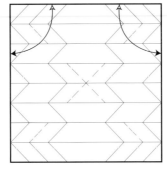

Crease between the 1/8ths by bisecting the corners.

24

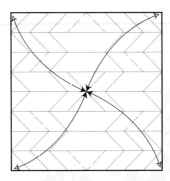

Crease between the 1/8ths by folding the corners to the centre.

25

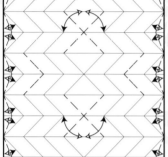

Fold the middle creases by folding the 1/8th crease to the creased point. Bisect the folds at the edges.

26

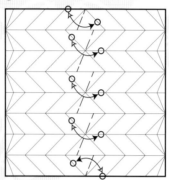

Match the diagonal crease onto the horizontal crease.

27

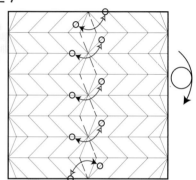

Match the diagonal crease onto the horizontal crease. Turn over.

28

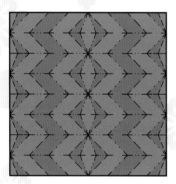

Collapse the crease pattern.

29

First to this stage.

30

Then all the way flat. Side B is complete. Open up both sides.

31

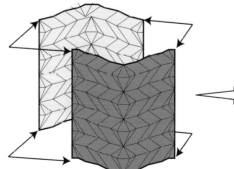

Use a strong tape to bind the edges of the two sheets.

32

Carefully collapse the folds of the taped model. The taped edge forms a crease.

33

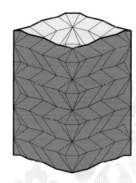

Expand the form to an opened state. The finished Tachi lampshade.

CREASE PATTERN SIDE A

Photocopy or trace and transfer this pattern onto your
material, then score and collapse.

CREASE PATTERN SIDE B

Photocopy or trace and transfer this pattern onto your
material, then score and collapse.

CREATING DISPLAYS

Origami models can become works of art. This section presents a range of amazing origami animals by Gen Hagiwara and demonstrates ways to mount the finished pieces, ready for display. You will also discover how to make foil-backed paper that is beautiful and easy to shape – perfect for bringing these creatures to life!

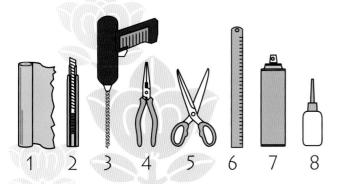

SUGGESTED TOOLS

Most of the tools and materials you will need are available in craft, hobby or hardware stores.

1. Aluminium foil
2. Utility knife
3. Drill
4. Pliers
5. Scissors
6. Steel ruler
7. Spray adhesive
8. PVA/Craft glue

DISPLAYING YOUR MODELS

There are many ways to display your finished models, including mobiles, natural mounts and block mounts. When creating a display, use your imagination! Try some of the following materials:

A. Natural elements such as branches, leaves and nuts give a natural feeling to the display.

B. Wooden blocks make elegant stands.

C. Wire is very versatile and cheap.

D. Needle and thread make hanging models.

Alternatively, you may prefer to use a ready-made display, such as:

E. Memo stand (available at stationery stores). Simply clip your origami onto the stand.

F. Display case (available at craft or hobby stores). Perfect to display your object while also keeping it safe from dust.

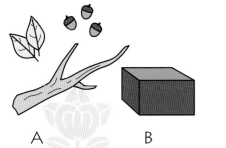

A　　　　　B

C

D

E

F

GOLDFISH

Goldfish are a popular family pet, loved for their bright colours. Try folding this model from duo-toned paper and make a collection of colourful fish to hang on a mobile.

SHEET SIZE: 15 × 15CM (5.9 × 5.9IN)
FINISHED SIZE: 9 × 5CM (3.54 × 1.96IN)
MODEL: GEN HAGIWARA
DIAGRAM: GEN HAGIWARA

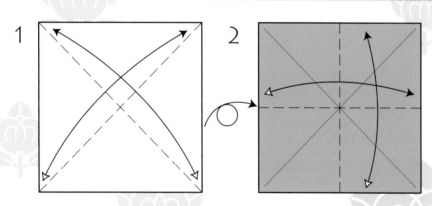

1 Begin white-side up. Fold and unfold diagonals, then turn over.

2 Book fold vertically and horizontally.

3 Fold the bottom edge to the diagonal and make a pinch at the end.

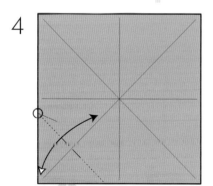

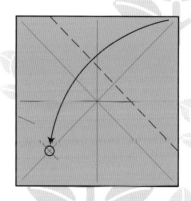

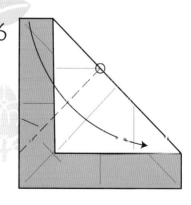

4 Pivot on the crease made in step 3 and make a pinch in the middle.

5 Fold the top-right corner to the crease made in step 4.

6 Fold the top-left corner down so the left-hand edge of the paper sits flush with the bottom of the triangle created in step 5.

7

Unfold steps 5 and 6.

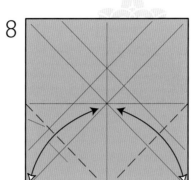

8

Fold the lower corners to the centre, then unfold. Turn over.

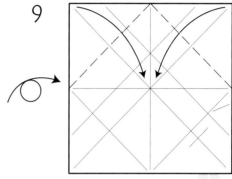

9

Blintz fold the top corners.

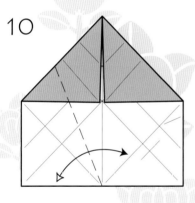

10

Fold and unfold the bottom edge to meet the opposite diagonal crease.

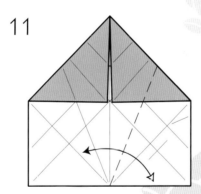

11

Fold and unfold the bottom edge to meet the opposite diagonal crease.

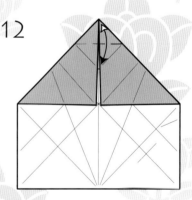

12

Crease the top triangle.

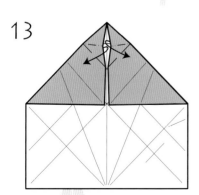

13

Open pockets and squash.

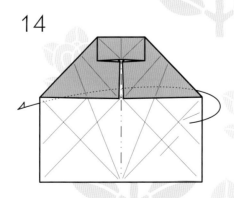

14

Fold the model in half horizontally.

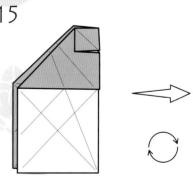

15

The model should look like this. Rotate to match step 16.

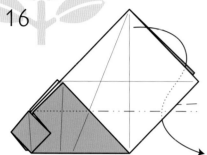

16

Inside reverse fold using existing creases.

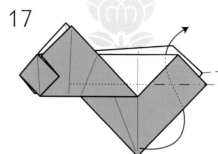

17

Inside reverse fold using existing creases.

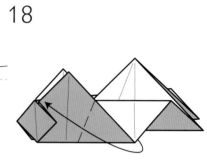

18

Fold the corner up at the existing crease.

19

Step 18 in progress.

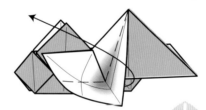

20

Squash down and flatten.

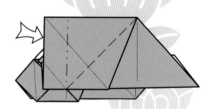

21

Open the pocket and squash.

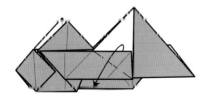

22

Fold the corner down.

23

Repeat steps 18–22 on the other side.

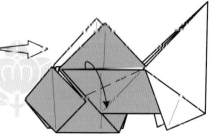

24

Fold the edge down to the crease.

25

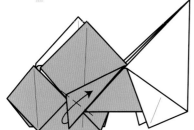

Fold the corner up.

26

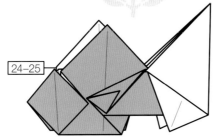

Repeat steps 24–25 on the other side.

27

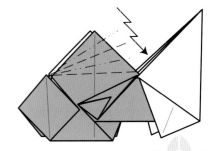

Pleat both layers.

28

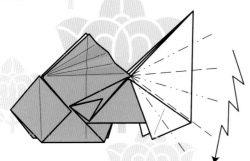

Pleat through all layers.

29

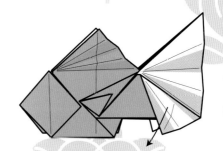

Open the tail fin.

30

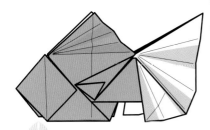

Completed goldfish.

MOBILE MOUNTING

1

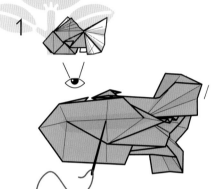

View from below. Make a hole in the centre with a needle.

2

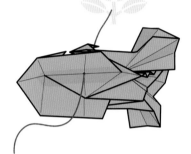

Run the thread through hole and up between the layers of the dorsal fin.

3

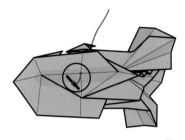

Tie a small stopper at the end of the string.

4

Apply a small amount of glue between the dorsal fins.

5

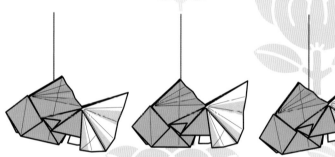

Adjust the angle of the goldfish by changing the position of the string.

6

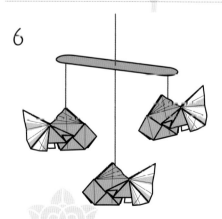

Assemble several fish into a mobile.

7

Or use a wire and block to create hanging display (see page 32).

SQUIRREL

This squirrel requires sculptural shaping at the end to bring out its full character. Try making your own foil-backed paper as described at the end of this model, and take your time folding to get the best results.

SHEET SIZE: 25 X 25CM (9.84 X 9.84IN)
FINISHED SIZE: 12 X 12CM (4.72 X 4.72IN)
MODEL: GEN HAGIWARA
DIAGRAM: GEN HAGIWARA

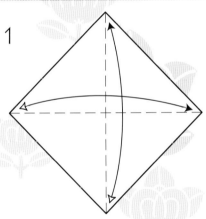

1

Begin white-side up. Fold and unfold diagonals.

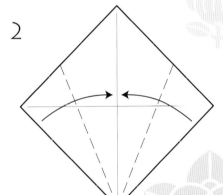

2

Fold lower edges up to the middle.

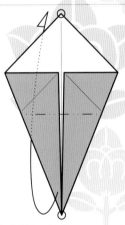

3

Mountain fold the bottom corner to the top corner.

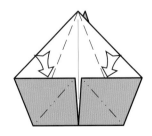

4

Squash fold both pockets.

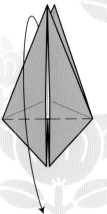

5

Fold down flap.

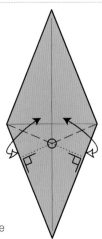

6

Pre-crease as shown.

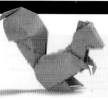

7

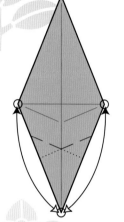

Pre-crease as shown.

8

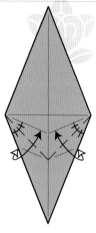

Pre-crease as shown.

9

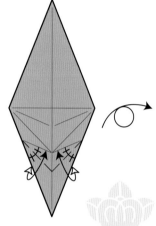

Pre-crease as shown. Turn over.

10

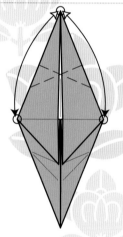

Pre-crease as shown.

11

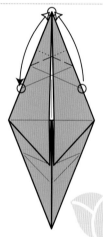

Pre-crease as shown.

12

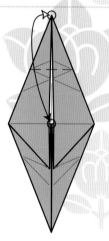

Pre-crease as shown.

13

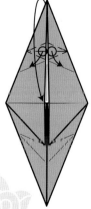

Fold down top corner and bring circled edge out.

14

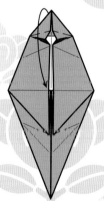

Step 13 in progress.

15

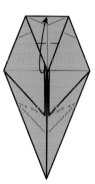

Fold the point up.

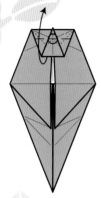

16

Fold up flap.

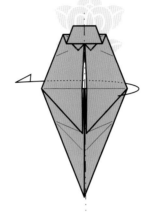

17

Mountain fold the model in half vertically.

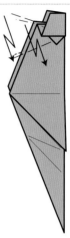

18

Crimp fold to shape the neck.

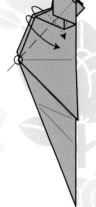

19

Valley fold the corner in front and repeat on the other side.

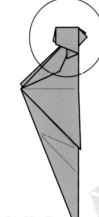

20

Steps 21–23 will focus on the head.

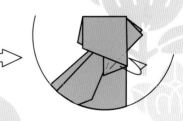

21

Mountain fold the corner inside. Repeat the on other side.

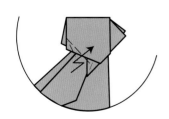

22

Pleat corners on both sides to form the mouth.

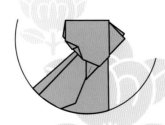

23

Step 22 completed.

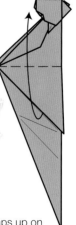

24

Fold flaps up on both sides.

25

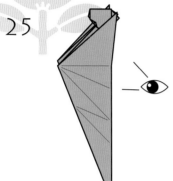

Gently open the model
and view from the back.

26

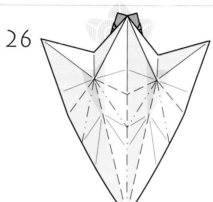

Prepare to collapse the model by shaping
the creases made in steps 6 and 8.

27

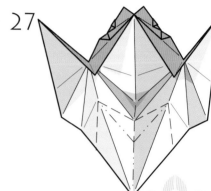

Collapse the model using the creases
made in steps 7 and 9.

28

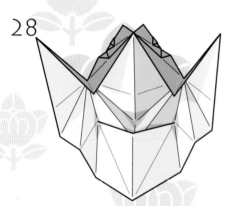

The collapse in progress. Completely collapse
and flatten the model, then view from the side.

29

Inside swivel fold. Repeat behind.

30

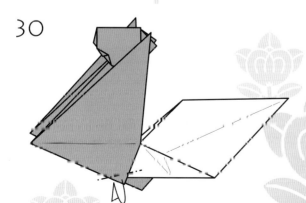

Mountain fold the corner. Repeat on
the other side.

31

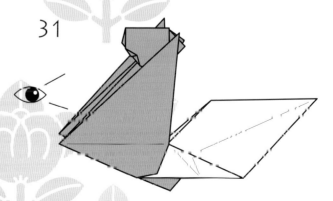

The following steps view the model
from the front.

32

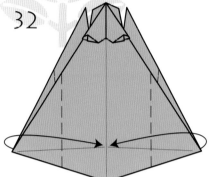

Fold the corners to the middle.

33

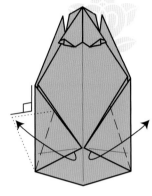

Fold the corners outwards.

34

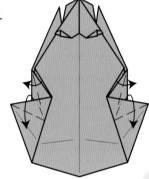

Swivel fold both sides.

35

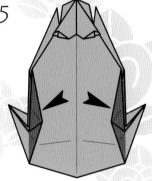

Create a closed sink in the shaded corners.

36

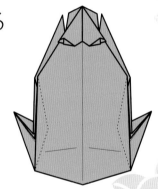

Sink completed. View the model from the side again.

37

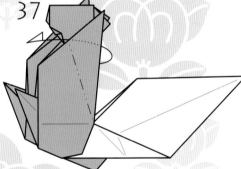

Mountain fold the flap. Repeat on the other side.

38

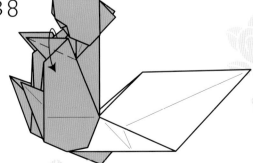

Fold the front leg in half. Repeat on the other side.

39

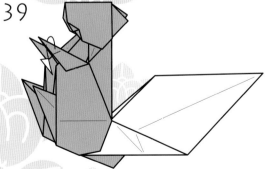

Mountain fold the corner of the leg. Repeat on the other side.

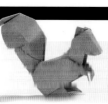

40

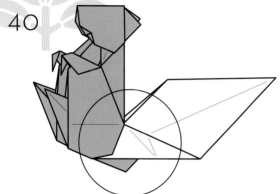

The following steps show an X-ray view inside the circle.

41

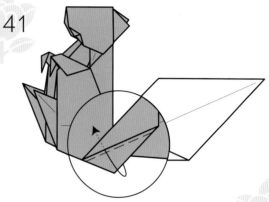

Tuck in the corner.

42

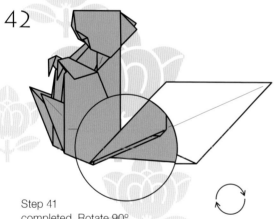

Step 41 completed. Rotate 90°.

43

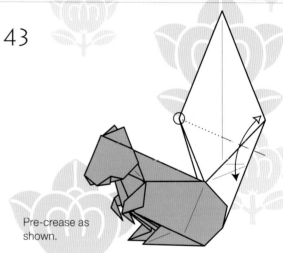

Pre-crease as shown.

44

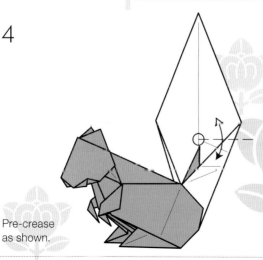

Pre-crease as shown.

45

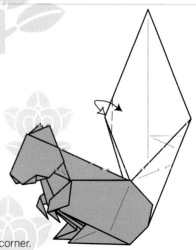

Fold and unfold the corner.

46

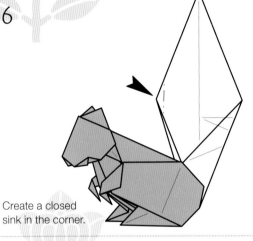

Create a closed
sink in the corner.

47

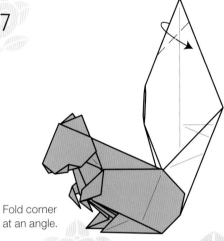

Fold corner
at an angle.

48

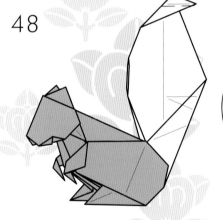

Tuck in the corner and lock the tip of the tail.

49

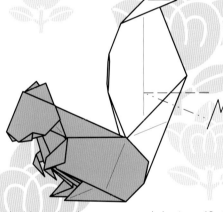

Pleat both sides using the creases made in steps 43–44.

50

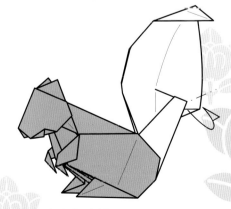

Fold in the edge to lock the folds.
Repeat on the other side.

51

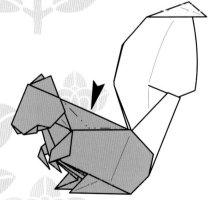

Push in the back.

52

Shape the body and tail.

53

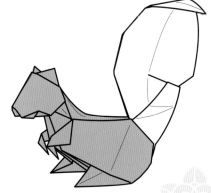

Completed squirrel.

54

The squirrel looks great in a ready-made display case. Try folding a squirrel from a sheet of foil-backed paper.

55

Alternatively, collect some leaves and acorns to make a natural setting.

56

Like this.

FOIL-BACKED PAPER

1

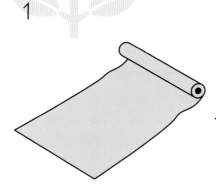

Spread a piece of aluminium foil onto a flat surface such as a table.

2

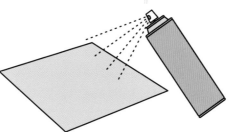

Spray adhesive lightly and evenly over the foil.

3

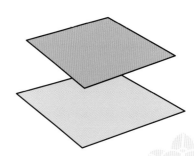

Place a sheet of paper on the foil. Wait for the adhesive to dry.

4

Step 3 completed. Turn over.

5

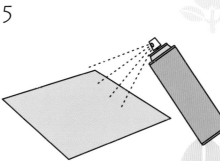

Spray adhesive lightly and evenly over the foil.

6

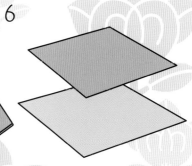

Place a second sheet of paper on the foil. Wait for the adhesive to dry.

7

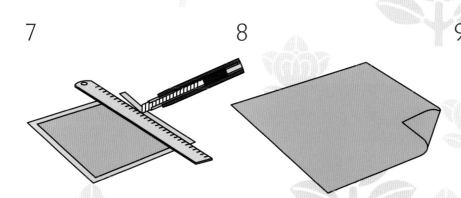

Trim the edges of the paper and foil, Measure and cut to make a square.

8

Completed foil-backed paper.

9

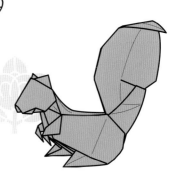

Foil-backed paper is used for models requiring lots of shaping, such as the squirrel.

FLYING SQUIRREL

A flying squirrel leaps from tree to tree, so try mounting your squirrel on a natural branch. The flying squirrel looks best when folded with paper that is the same colour on each side.

SHEET SIZE: 25 X 25CM (9.84 X 9.84IN)
FINISHED SIZE: 5 X 9CM (1.96 X 3.54IN)
MODEL: GEN HAGIWARA
DIAGRAM: GEN HAGIWARA

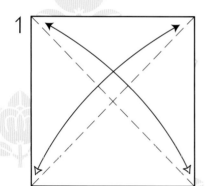

1

Begin white-side up.
Fold and unfold diagonals.

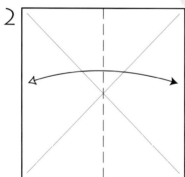

2

Book fold and unfold vertically.

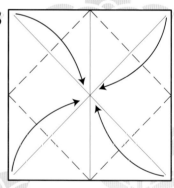

3

Blintz fold all corners to the centre.

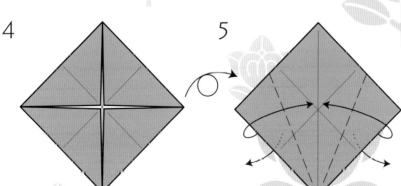

4

Step 3 completed.
Turn over.

5

Fold lower edges to the middle and bring the layer behind to the front.

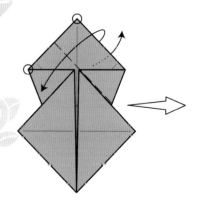

6

Fold top edge and bring the layer behind to the front.

7

Squash fold and bring the layer behind to the front

8

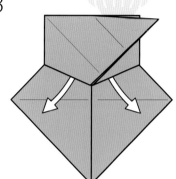

Pull out the flaps.

9

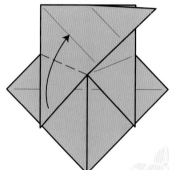

Valley fold the flap up.

10

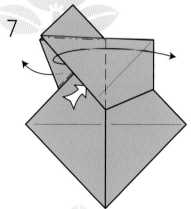

Fold the flap to the other side.

11

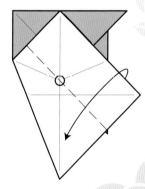

Fold at the intersection of the creases.

12

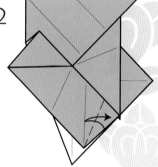

Fold the edge to the crease and unfold. Undo step 10 to 12 and return to the shape of step 10.

13

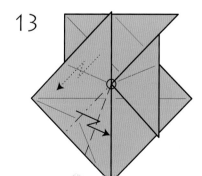

Pleat the lower section and swivel the top section outwards.

14

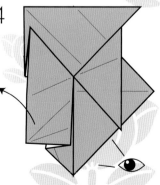

Lift the corner lightly and view the model from the side.

15

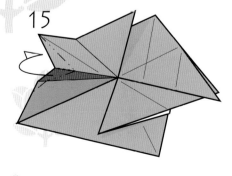

Inside reverse fold on the creases made in step 12 and then flatten.

16

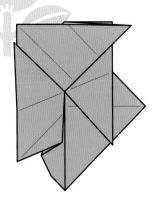

Step 15 completed. The model lies flat again.

17

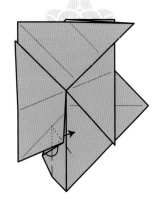

Inside reverse fold.

18

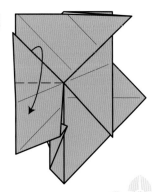

Fold the flap down.

19

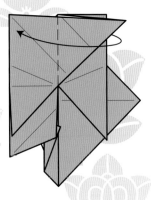

Fold the flap to the other side.

20

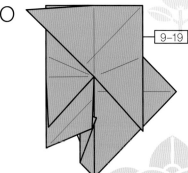

9–19

Repeat steps 9–19 on other side.

21

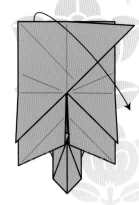

Fold the corner down.

22

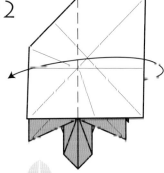

Fold the flap to the other side.

23

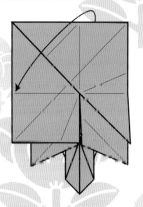

Fold the corner down.

24

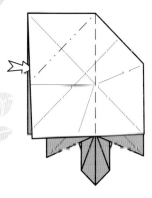

Squash fold.

25

Fold the flap to the other side.

26

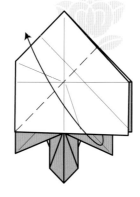

Fold the flap up on the existing crease.

27

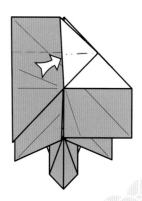

Squash fold.

28

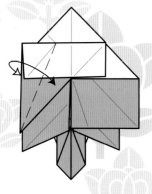

Valley fold the corner and unfold.

29

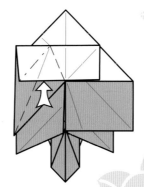

Squash fold.

30

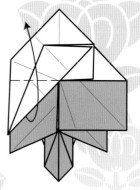

Fold the flap up.

31

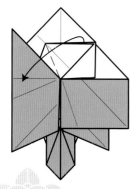

Fold the flap down.

32

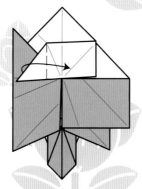

Valley fold.

33

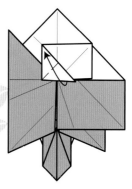

Valley fold.

34

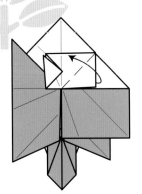

Valley fold.

35

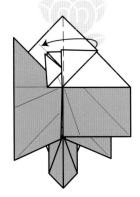

Fold the flap to the other side.

36

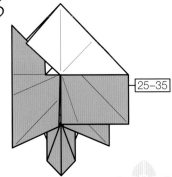

25–35

Repeat steps 25–35 on the other side.

37

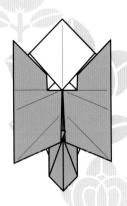

Steps 25–35 are complete. Turn over.

38

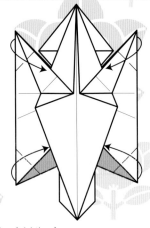

Squash fold on both sides and bring the edges to the middle.

39

Valley fold the four corners.

40

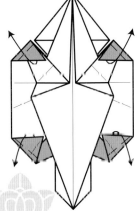

Valley fold the four corners.

41

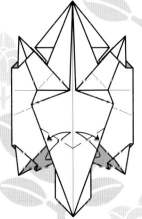

Pre-crease the base of the tail.

42

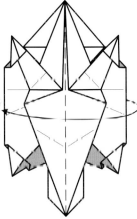

Valley fold in half vertically.

43

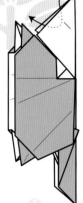

Inside reverse fold the corner.

44

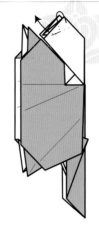

Inside reverse fold both corners.

45

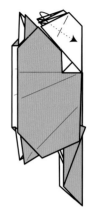

Tuck in the middle corner.

46

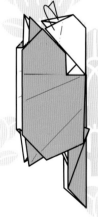

Fold in both corners.

47

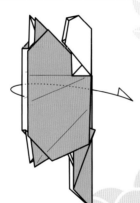

Open up the body.

48

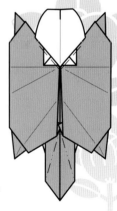

Fold the ears up and shape the tail.

49

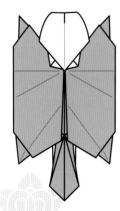

The tail is now shaped.

50

Completed flying squirrel.

NATURAL MOUNT

1

Using pliers, straighten a wire and cut off a 20cm (7.8in) length.

2

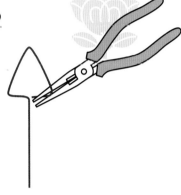

Bend the wire into the shape of a triangle the same size as the squirrel's head.

3

Bend the neck.

4

Shape the head part as shown.

5

Find a stable piece of wood or branch that is heavy enough to hold the model.

6

Drill a hole in the wood the same size as the gauge of the wire.

7

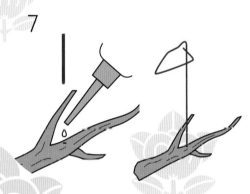

Put a drop of glue in the hole then insert the wire into the hole.

8

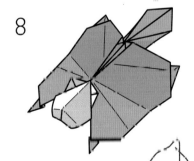

Place the model onto the wire.

9

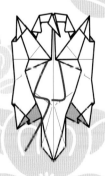

Insert the triangle into the gap behind the head.

10

The completed model is now ready for display.

KANGAROO

This kangaroo is flexible in posture so you can try several different poses and make a big family for your mantelpiece. Try mounting your kangaroo family on a series of wooden blocks.

SHEET SIZE: 30 X 30CM (11.81 X 11.81IN)
FINISHED SIZE: 15 X 8CM (5.90 X 3.14IN)
MODEL: GEN HAGIWARA
DIAGRAM: GEN HAGIWARA

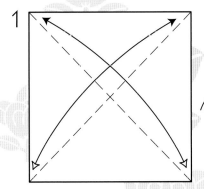

1 Begin white-side up. Fold and unfold the diagonals. Turn over.

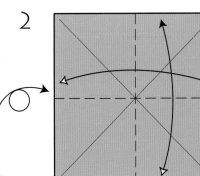

2 Book fold and unfold vertically and horizontally.

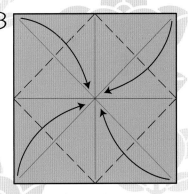

3 Fold all corners to the centre.

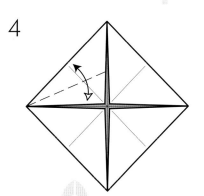

4 Fold the edge to the outer edge.

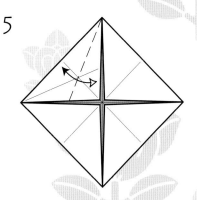

5 Fold the edge to the outer edge.

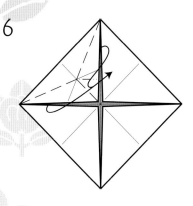

6 Rabbit-ear fold.

7

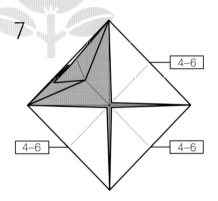

Repeat steps 4–6 on the other three corners.

8

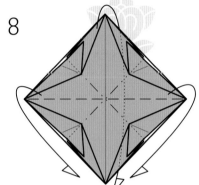

Bring the three corners down to meet the bottom corner.

9

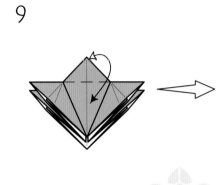

Fold and unfold the top triangle.

10

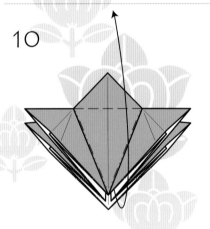

Petal fold.

11

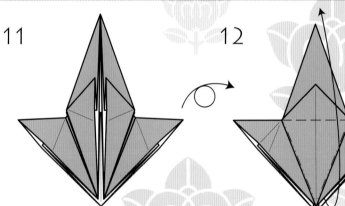

Step 10 completed. Turn over.

12

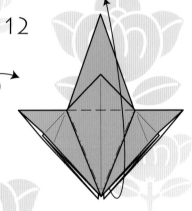

Petal fold.

13

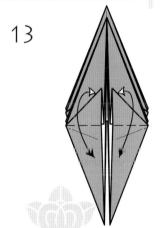

Fold down the flaps and unfold.

14

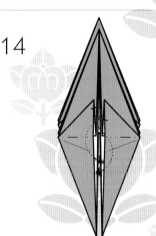

Inside reverse fold the flaps.

15

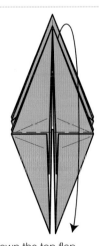

Fold down the top flap.

16

Fold the flap to the other side.

17

Fold the flap up on existing crease.

18

Squash fold.

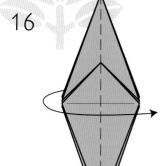

19

Repeat step 17–18 on the other side.

17–18

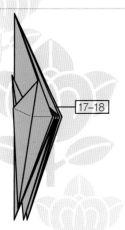

20

Steps 21–26 will focus on the circled area.

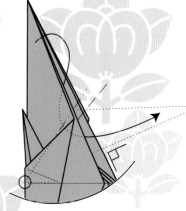

21

Inside reverse fold.

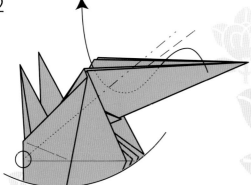

22

Inside reverse fold.

23

Pleat both sides.

24

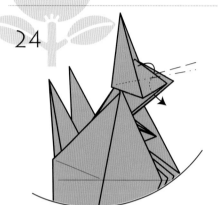

Inside reverse fold the middle corner.

25

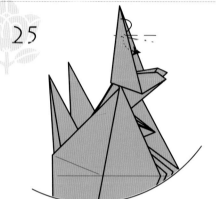

Inside reverse fold the tip.

26

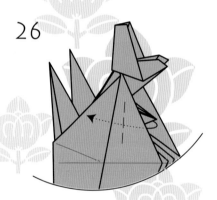

Tuck in the corner inside.

27

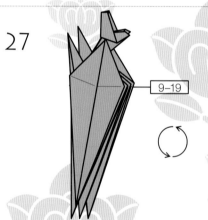

9–19

Repeat steps 9–19 on the other side. Rotate the model 90°.

28

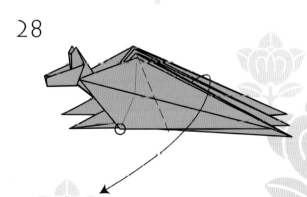

Valley fold, bringing the edge to the circled corner.

29

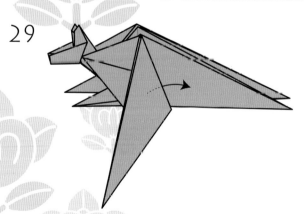

Bring the paper out from behind.

30

Mountain fold the corner inside.

31

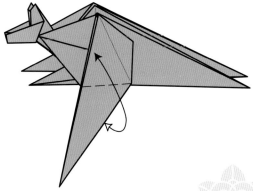

Fold and unfold.

32

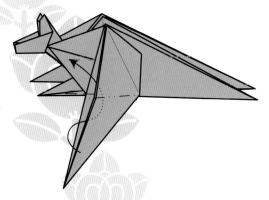

Inside reverse fold at the second pocket from the front using the creases made in step 31.

33

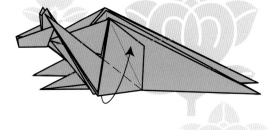

Valley fold and open up the flap.

34

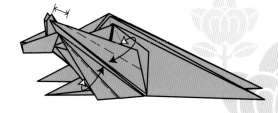

Fold the edges to the middle then unfold.
Note: the folds don't intersect the point.

35

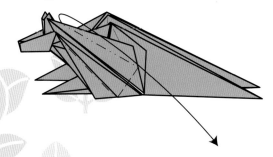

Petal fold.

36

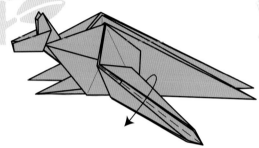

Close the leg.

37

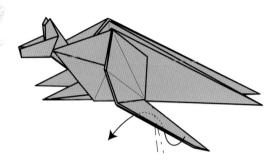

Inside reverse fold.

38

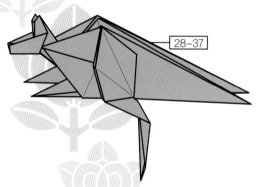

28–37

Repeat steps 28–37 on the other side.

39

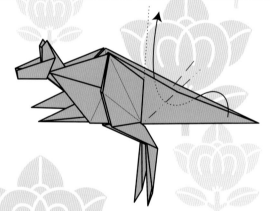

Inside reverse fold the tail.

40

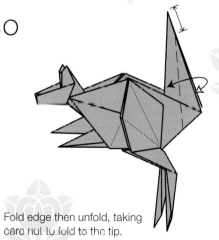

Fold edge then unfold, taking care not to fold to the tip.

41

Inside swivel fold.

42

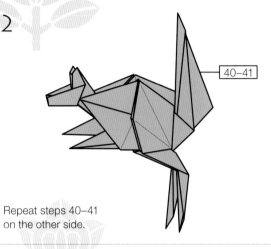

40–41

Repeat steps 40–41
on the other side.

43

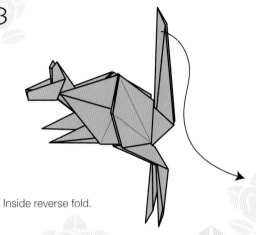

Inside reverse fold.

44

Inside reverse fold.

45

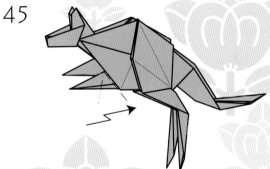

Crimp the arm.

46

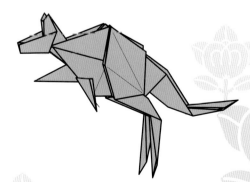

Like this. Repeat on the other side.

47

Tuck in the corners on both sides.

48

Curve the neck.

49

Valley fold the ears outwards from the head.
Rotate slightly so the kangaroo is in mid-jump.

50

The kangaroo is complete.

51

Different poses are possible with this
design. Try out some variations.

52

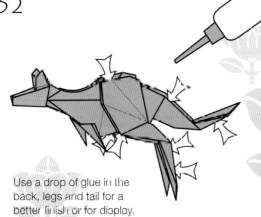

Use a drop of glue in the
back, legs and tail for a
better finish or for display.

BLOCK MOUNT TYPE 1

1

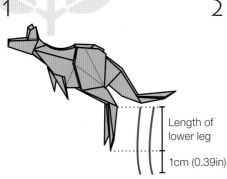

Length of
lower leg

1cm (0.39in)

Cut two lengths of wire 1cm (0.39in)
longer than the lower part of the leg.

2

Open up each leg.

3

Apply glue between the layers.

4

Place a length of wire in each leg.

5

Close the folds on each leg and wait
for the glue to dry.

6

The model should look like this.

7

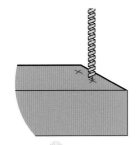

Drill two holes in a wooden block. The
holes should be the same size as the
gauge of the wire.

8

Apply a drop of glue into the holes,
then insert the wire into the holes.

9

Completed mounting of the kangaroo.

BLOCK MOUNT TYPE 2

1

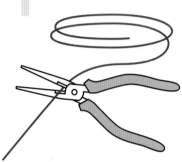

Straighten and cut a length of wire. The length will be the height of the mount.

2

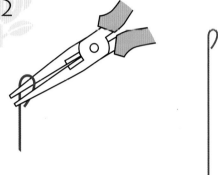

Make small loop at the end of the wire.

3

Drill a hole into a wooden block. The hole should be the same size as the gauge of the wire.

4

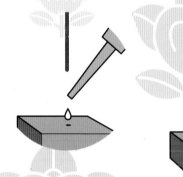

Put a drop of glue into the hole and then insert the wire.

5

Insert the wire loop into the body between the layers

6

Completed mounting of the kangaroo